Change Your Mind

I dedicate this book, with profound gratitude and appreciation, to who I AM in Essence and to ALL-THAT-IS and to Michaela and Gabriella, whom I love deeply.

To Kate
I honour your
wisdom, sheer
beauty & utter
magnificence
with deep gratitude
Johanna

CHANGE
YOUR
MIND

How to benefit from
our negative emotions and
intimately connect
with our Essence

JOHANNA CLARITEE

First published in the United Kingdom in 2010
by Onawa Publishing

ISBN 978-0-9565404-0-9

Produced by
The Choir Press
www.thechoirpress.co.uk

Contents

Preface

Change Your Mind discusses a great many things and yet just one topic. Although it contains nothing that we don't already know somewhere, somehow in the deepest recesses of our being, chances are that we have lost sight of part or all of it or we have not yet accessed it, at least not from this angle. Don't put the book down just yet. Even if you have come across some of the ideas – although many perspectives and concepts are novel and extremely effective – this material will facilitate further integration or assimilation. If the book works for you, you will find it extremely powerful, effective and worthwhile. So, what in particular does *Change Your Mind* deal with?

This book is concerned with emotions such as anger, frustration, worry, doubt, guilt, fear and powerlessness, which we are generally not so keen on and usually want to experience less of. It is also about emotions such as contentment, enthusiasm, joy, exuberance and freedom, which we generally would like to experience more of. In essence, the first part of the book is about the significance, value and scope of our feelings, the welcome and the unwelcome ones. It is about using our emotions to our maximum advantage. Our emotions are immensely revealing and helpful in nature and they are an enormously effective route to heightened clarity and awareness. We may utilise our feelings to guide us away from those viewpoints, notions or beliefs which are not working for us, and towards those which are much more helpful and more conducive to achieving our most intrinsic intent and most cherished desires. In doing so we decrease the experience of emotional pain and unpleasant feelings and increase the experience of enthusiasm and freedom in our life. A natural consequence of this is that we operate more on course with who we are in Essence or at the Core.

The book also offers several techniques to proactively promote a more profound and intimate relationship and connection with our Essence or Intrinsic Self. In practising these methods we get in touch with our inherent source of immense peace, fulfilment, security, clarity, understanding, elation and freedom, which our Core Aspect personifies. Using one or several of these techniques we experience those qualities in a more prominent way and on a more regular basis.

In addition to the above-mentioned potent processes and tools, *Change Your Mind* also offers copious food for thought, a multitude of helpful perspectives and unusual ideas and concepts. It is full of valuable pointers and in many ways uplifting and inspirational. The language of the book is jargon-free and straight to the point.

The content of the book is my understanding and truth, what I found to be so. The processes and techniques which I developed en route, and the understanding and clarity which they afforded me, grew out of close observations of myself and others, my impassioned and intense yearning to move past the restrictions, struggles and dissatisfactions of my life, and my strong desire to achieve greater ease and freedom. Applying those methods brought me from the experience of monumental emotional pain, anger, resentment, frustration, restlessness and low self-esteem, to a place of tremendously increased ease, joy, sense of worth, confidence, enthusiasm, purpose and colossal internal freedom. Only now do I fully realise and appreciate the immensity of my previous limitations and suffering and the part I played in creating them. Back then, although dissatisfied and unhappy, it seemed a pretty normal place to be. And yet, I was restless and compelled to find a way out.

My experiences and my journey fuelled my great intent and passion to gain for myself and to facilitate for others to the highest degree, increased clarity, empowerment and liberation from all that holds us back from being who we want to be and can be. In addition, I found it infinitely worthwhile, fascinating and exhilarating to discover the world inside of me and to become more connected and intimate with who I am at the Core of my Being.

It is my ardent intention for you, the reader of this book, to gain powerfully from the understanding and tools offered and for you to get to know more intimately the Essence of your being, the You, which is immensely beautiful, wise, aware, graceful, joyful, peaceful, powerful and totally free. I invite you to embark on a fascinating journey of discovery and empowerment. Allow yourself to be swept along to discover the stupendous, breathtaking, magnificent, radiant pearl inside of you.

Part 1

Our emotions and
their enormous significance
and value

1.1 Key aspects of our emotions

a) The characteristics of emotions

Within the context of this book I use the terms emotions, feelings and moods interchangeably. Emotions which we gladly experience and enjoy such as optimism, enthusiasm, passion, empowerment, serenity and joy, I label as **'positive'** emotions. Uncomfortable, unpleasant, unwelcome emotions such as pessimism, frustration, disappointment, worry, discouragement, anger, jealousy, insecurity, guilt, fear or despair, I call **'negative'**. Emotions are basically energy fluctuations in our body and mind. The energy fluctuations are experienced in our body as symptoms such as stomach tension, increased heart rate, faster breathing, elevated blood pressure, dizziness, numbness and tightening of our chest – anything from minor discomfort to severe discomfort. In our mind we may be aware of racing thoughts, confusion, increased turbulence or just dullness and a reduced sense of aliveness. According to their energy and experienced sensations we classify emotions as sadness, anger, joy, frustration, boredom, excitement, anxiety, fear and enthusiasm, amongst others.

Each type of emotion has its own specific energy pattern. Energy can be depicted pictorially as the pattern of a uniform wave.

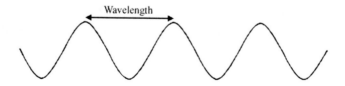

In energy terms the distance between two adjacent wave peaks is called a wavelength and the number of waves per unit time is defined as frequency. Energy moving or vibrating with a short wavelength and high frequency is termed as high energy. Energy moving with a long wavelength and low frequency is classified as low energy.

Elated, good-feeling emotions have a higher frequency and a finer, more subtle energy than less welcome or so-called negative emotions. The wavelength or frequency of our emotions encompasses a wide spectrum of energy:

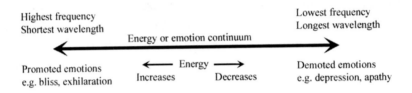

Our emotions may be deliberately promoted or demoted. Factors which promote or demote our Energy-in-**motion** are discussed later. First I want to focus on what sets our emotions in motion.

b) How our emotions are generated

o   First something happens. We are involved in a situation, we observe a behaviour or attitude, somebody makes a comment or judgement or our thoughts dart to some circumstances in the past or expected future.

o   In response to the observed we decide what the incident or comment means. We form an opinion or make a judgement; we have some thoughts on the matter. This may happen consciously i.e. we are aware of what we are thinking. We may even deliberately choose to view the occurrence in a particular way. Alternatively, we may not be aware of our thought processes; we may be unaware that we have adopted a viewpoint and/or we may be unconscious of the content of the adopted viewpoint or perspective.

o In response to our adopted perspective or thoughts we become angry, happy, upset, disappointed, peaceful, overwhelmed, anxious, elated. This is the crucial part. **Our feelings are set in motion as a result of the meaning we have given something. It is not the incident, comment or attitude that makes us feel bad or good, comfortable or uncomfortable. It is how we view the incident that determines how we feel.**

Most of us have seen somebody getting upset, angry, frustrated or disappointed over something, which seemed pretty trivial to us. Or we have noticed a group of people reacting to the same event in many different ways. The reason for this is that it is not the event which makes us feel a particular way, but it is the meaning we give the event that causes us to feel happy or sad, peaceful or anxious, disappointed or pleased.

c) So, what makes an emotion pleasant or uncomfortable?

Whether a feeling is comfortable or uncomfortable depends on whether the perspective or opinion we have adopted is beneficial or detrimental with regard to our overall well-being. Our emotions are an indication of how on-course or off-course our thinking is with our deepest desires, our most cherished goals and intentions.

Those thoughts causing **negative** emotions are out of sync with the Core of our Being. They are an indication that the perspective, idea, conclusion or attitude we have chosen now, or in the past and activated now, is restricting or diminishing us. Our adopted notion is denying the larger truth of who we are.

Those thoughts causing **positive** emotions e.g. elation, exhilaration, excitement, joy, peace, well-being, freedom or ease are compatible with the way of being of our Authentic Self. When we feel 'positive' emotions we are aligned with or operating from the level of our Core Self. We are thinking and acting in keeping with our innermost intentions.

The worse we feel, the more detrimental to our well-being is the perspective we are holding or the meaning we have given. The better we feel the more on-course our viewpoint is with those held at the Core of our Being.

d) Some additional factors which demote or promote our emotional well-being

In addition to harbouring an idea or perspective which is not in our best interests and which does not reflect our larger truth, we may also lower to some degree our feel-good factor by imbalance in any area of our life. We may **demote** our comfort by:

o Not taking appropriate care of our body such as ingesting food or drinks which harm our body, or through insufficient rest, insufficient movement, insufficient exposure to natural light or by breathing poor quality air and so on.
o Not supportively stimulating our mind e.g. by doing what bores us or alienates us, by lack of exposure to uplifting material (literature, music, art) or by subjecting it to depressing material or not engaging our intellect at all.
o Not responding to our spiritual needs.
   In short, imbalance in any of our areas.

Our emotions or feel-good factor may be **promoted** by rectifying any of the above and by anything that aligns us more with our Essence. Some examples are:

o Changing our mind and adopting a more beneficial thought or belief.
o Improving our physical health through e.g. exercise, supportive food, sufficient rest.
o Stilling our mind.
o Doing what interests, excites, inspires or enthuses us.

More extensive examples are given in part 3.

e) Promoting our emotions may proceed gradually

Although we may dramatically raise our emotions instantly in the face of a momentous shift in perspective, most commonly our emotions are promoted through a series of stages. Usually, to get from depression to exhilaration we have to move through a series of emotions such as anger, doubt, frustration, hopefulness, enthusiasm, peace. In other words we work our way up. Each step up is achieved by finding a more beneficial notion. For example when we are depressed we might think "There is no point in this". However, subsequently we may adopt the idea "This is out of order" or "I am not having this" and get angry. We may then move into doubt with "Maybe this has something to do with me" or "Maybe I can do something about it". After that, we might become first hopeful and then enthusiastic and decide that we can and will do something about it and make it work for us. Then we become inspired and elated by the prospects. Our thoughts or viewpoints raise us up every step of the way.

1.2 The significance and implications of the choice of our perspectives

With regard to our emotions, the perspective we adopt is decisive. Therefore let's look more closely into our choice of perspective and its relevance as to how we experience our life and world.

a) Diagrammatic illustration of what perspective means

An occurrence or subject may be viewed from many different angles.

Diagrams to illustrate various views of the
same objects as seen from different perspectives

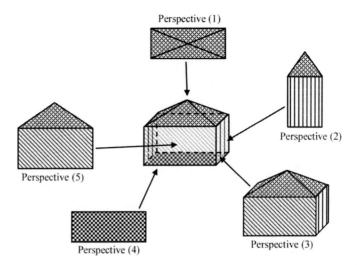

Perspective (1)

Perspective (2)

Perspective (5)

Perspective (4)

Perspective (3)

Most occurrences may be viewed from many different angles or perspectives. Out of the pool of available perspectives we usually – either consciously or unconsciously – choose a particular 'angle' or perspective and the chosen angle or meaning will form our reality.

Once we have chosen a viewpoint it becomes part of our 'filter' through which we view the world until one day we change our mind and disregard the old perspective and adopt a new one. So how do we choose the meaning we give something?

b) How we choose a particular perspective

o In line with perspectives chosen previously in similar contexts or circumstances. We opt for the same view again and again.

o Or line with choices made by others. We may choose the perspective or interpretation adopted by one other person, a group of people such as our family circle, friends or colleagues or according to the prevailing judgements of a community or the predominant views of a particular group of the population. Sometimes others may offer their perspective quite intensively, forcefully or persistently.

o Or according to our strong inner gut-level instinct or knowing. We trust what we instinctively know in preference to our own mental arguments or the influences of others.

o Or after thorough deliberation or comprehensive investigation or in-depth reflection or quiet contemplation. We give the situation some thought and deliberately choose a perspective. Sometimes we arrive at a place of great clarity instantly or without much reflection.

o Or we choose a particular perspective **unconsciously**, without being fully aware that we are making an interpretation. It may seem as if we are just observing what is so and we are not in any way contributing,

o Or we choose **consciously**, in which case we are fully aware of what we are doing and we are clear that we are making a choice and nothing but a choice.

The perspective we adopt is either of **benefit** to and in line with who we want to be and on course with who we are in Essence or **counterproductive** to achieving our most sacred wishes and off-course with who we are at the Core. It is either helping or hindering

c) Some of the factors involved in the choosing of a
   perspective:

o *Our level of understanding and awareness*
   The greater our level of awareness and clarity, the more extensive is the reservoir of perspectives available to us to choose from. In addition, the greater our awareness, the greater our discerning power with regard to which perspectives are beneficial to us and which are not.

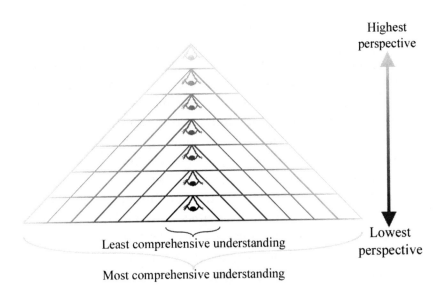

Highest perspective

Lowest perspective

Least comprehensive understanding

Most comprehensive understanding

The higher our viewing point is, the more comprehensive is our understanding and the clearer we are as to the value of a particular perspective and its effects. How we may cultivate greater levels of awareness and understanding is discussed in Part 3.

○ *Which part of us is dominant at the time.*
Sometimes different parts or aspects within us (I call them Ego parts; more in Part 2) hold different, occasionally directly opposing perspectives with respect to the same scenario and on different occasions one of our aspects has the upper hand and on another occasion or just a minute later another part, representing an alternative perspective, is in the driver's seat. For example, one day we may see the comment of a friend as a light-hearted joke; in another instance we may consider the same remark as insensitive or offensive and on another occasion we will judge the comment differently still. If we are aware enough to realise which of our parts is acting out, we can then intervene and purposefully place a part with a more beneficial viewpoint in the driver's seat. In general, the more in touch we are with our Essence, the more beneficial a perspective we will choose.

○ *The degree of our willingness to be open-minded and to consider alternative viewpoints*
The more we are prepared to explore and consider alternative views, and the more we appreciate that something may be viewed from a different, maybe more helpful angle, the greater the variety of perspectives available to us to choose from. In addition, the more open-minded we are, the more easily and readily we change our mind in the face of a more advantageous perspective.

○ *The magnitude of past investment in a particular perspective*
A particular notion or belief may have been adopted a great number of times in the past and with time a considerable amount of emotional charge such as fear may have accumulated around that particular viewpoint. When an event activates such a belief, the magnetism and emotional force that this belief exerts makes it more difficult to step back from the triggering scenario, harder to disengage from the emotional turmoil and more challenging to consider or

adopt an alternative perspective, unless we are quite profi-
cient in stepping back from a triggering thought and we are
armed with an arsenal of empowering perspectives from
which to select a more beneficial viewpoint. How to
proceed, when we are in the grip of a highly charged belief,
is described in detail in the process (1.6).

o *The effect of a cluster of beliefs*
   Sometimes, a triggered notion or belief forms part of a
   cluster of beliefs with one idea linked to another, more basic
   idea, which in turn is associated with a further, more
   cardinal judgement. If we follow the link or thread of the
   coupled convictions as described in the process (1.6), we
   eventually arrive at the core belief, which is usually one of
   the most detrimental, disabling, influential beliefs in the
   chain of thoughts and the one which we are least aware of,
   unless we are in the habit of reflectively observing our
   feelings and thoughts. Thus a fairly innocuous belief may be
   highly charged, intense or strongly defended because of the
   hugely dysfunctional underlying beliefs associated with it.
       In both this and the case above, because of the strong
   magnetic power of the belief, we are more inclined to choose
   the well-established, highly charged perspective again.

o *Our willingness to take responsibility for the perspective we
   choose*
   If we accept full ownership of our viewpoints and what we
   think, then we will want to instantly intervene when an
   uncomfortable feeling has made us aware that we entertain a
   less beneficial idea or thought, and we will want to think a
   more beneficial thought.
       In general, we will want to reflect and give some thought
   to how we view what we observe, the situations or events,
   the relationships or dynamics we notice and pay attention to.
   We will want to be aware of our viewpoint, should we have
   adopted one unconsciously. Alternatively, when faced with
   an incident or situation, we choose consciously and deliber-

ately a perspective in line with our principles and values. Thus we act as conscious and aware creators of our experiences.

Whatever may influence our choice of perspective, we always may override any factors and intervene with an independent, purposeful, conscious choice.

Our emotions of comfort or discomfort will always inform us as to how beneficial or otherwise the perspective is that we have opted for.

e) The cycle of perspective and resultant sponsored belief and the ensuing experience

I cannot stress enough that our experiences are generated by our interpretations of events and our interpretations are often guided by our already existing beliefs.

This is how it starts and is perpetuated:

1) At the beginning there is an event.
2) We give the event its meaning; we make an interpretation. When we make the same interpretation repeatedly in response to similar situations, then the chosen meaning develops into a belief. The more often we opt for the same viewpoint, the more entrenched the belief becomes.
3) In response to the resultant experienced emotion we may:
   • make use of our feelings to become fully aware of the belief we have adopted or re-adopted or
   • without full awareness maintain the previously chosen belief. In this case the process becomes or remains circular.

Unless we use our uncomfortable feelings to become aware of a detrimental idea we have adopted and unless we acknowledge ourselves as the selector of the notion, the process becomes circular and we have the same recurring experiences. Only by allowing ourselves to become conscious of our thoughts and beliefs and by owning them and through choosing, where advisable, an alternative, more beneficial, 'good-feeling' notion are we able to exit a particular perpetual cycle.

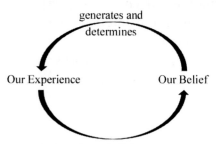

a) gives rise to belief or
b) confirms and reinforces an established belief or
c) an observation is made; no conclusion is drawn or belief formed

In essence we sculpture our experiences and our development by the perspectives and notions we adopt and where we place our attention.

1.3 Implications of the relationship between the adopted perspective and the resultant experience

The fact that our emotions are set in motion by what we think puts us in charge of our experiences. The onus for how we feel is firmly in our court; by controlling what we think we control how we feel. **We can change at any stage how we feel by choosing a different perspective or thought.** If we are aware that our thoughts affect how we feel, we can purposefully intervene. We may consciously and deliberately choose a viewpoint or idea which causes us to feel better. If we are not aware of this we may still change our perspective and thus our feelings for a whole range of other reasons. Maybe we are inspired by what somebody said or did or maybe we respond to an instinctive impulse. Yet we can always consciously choose a viewpoint which makes us at least feel a little bit more comfortable. Moreover, if we give everything its meaning, we might as well choose meanings which serve us well; meanings which bring us relief from suffering and increased freedom, peace, fulfilment, empowerment and expansion.

We decide how our energy is put into motion, whatever the circumstances. Even if a large number of people or the whole world judge a particular behaviour or remark offensive, it still does not mean that we have to do so. We cannot hide behind other people's choices or use them to deny our own responsibility for what we choose. We always have a choice of what we make of an event and our interpretation, however justifiable we find it, causes us to feel glad, angry, elated, stressed, relieved, disappointed, exhilarated.

Within a sample spectrum of comments from others ranging from an innocent, completely non-provocative remark, made with the utmost consideration and care, which hardly anybody would consider offensive, to the most vile, verbally aggressive and provocative attack, which most people would object to, we can take offence or not take offence at either end of the spectrum. We may object to the most benign, considerate, friendly remark due to our interpretation or we can remain totally centred, at ease, peaceful in the face of the most aggressive posture and most forceful and foul outpouring, due to the choice of the meaning and perspective we have adopted.

It is important to bear in mind that whatever another person says or does is a display of his/her mental world. He/she offers us a glimpse into part of his/her reality, into some of his/her adopted beliefs or attitudes. What somebody says has singularly to do with his/her choices and nothing to do with us. However, what we make of what that particular person said or did has everything to do with us. It is our choice and our responsibility and ours alone. Even if the action or comment was offered with the intention to hurt (and often it is not, only our assumptions make it hurtful), then it is still up to us whether we reactively comply with the intention or proactively choose a different stance and thus intentionally decide how we are going to experience the 'appalling, spiteful' incident. It is up to our choice of perspective whether we feel hurt or peaceful, whether we lose or gain from the event.

We may employ our emotions as valuable messengers. We may use an uncomfortable feeling as a signal that we entertain a perspective or notion, which is detrimental to our overall well-being or out of touch with who we are at our Core. The more incompatible our outlook or idea is with those of our Essence, the more awful we feel. Once we appreciate the enormous informative character of our emotion we may welcome any uncomfortable feelings and use them to our advantage. We employ our feelings to discover those thoughts and ideas we are unaware of and to place us in a position to make informed conscious choices.

Given that we and we alone choose the perspective or inter-pretation we adopt, we might as well purposefully choose those perspectives which benefit us, which are on course with who we want to be. In my opinion it is extremely worthwhile to give our choices some thought and ensure that we do not take on board the perspectives of others without reflection and deliberation.

The meaning we give something is our responsibility and ours alone. The meaning others adopt is their responsibility. However, it is our responsibility to clarify for others the meaning we attach to a particular comment, action, situation or relationship. We must ensure that the other is clear what we mean by what we say. Equally it is up to us to check out what the other means by what they say.

Our interpretations are creative. They create our experi-ence. There is a dance between meaning and experience and the cycle continues, until we purposefully intervene with reflective awareness. Past meanings lead to present interpreta-tions and experiences, which in turn induce future interpretations and experiences, unless we start to observe our thoughts and become aware of the meaning we have given something. Once we realise the idea that we have taken on board, we can change our mind, if the notion is not helpful, and thus we intervene in the cycle of experience and meaning and ensure, that we do not have the same undesirable experi-ence again and again.

1.4 Some further points regarding emotions

Emotions may be used as a tool for manipulation or control, either consciously or unconsciously. For example, although anger may be used as a driving force to achieve an objective, it can equally be used as a powerful means to intimidate or cajole those who see themselves as timid or sensitive. It can be quite effective against those who allow it to be. We may purposefully use the demonstration of disappointment, indignation, disapproval, jealousy or self-pity as a method to influence others. For example, disappointment can easily induce feelings of guilt in those who are prone to seek approval of others. However, it is important to bear in mind that the person who is using anger, disappointment, hurt etc. manipulatively, is acting from a position of feeling powerless or judging him/herself unable to achieve his/her objective, otherwise he/she would not resort to the use of those tools. He/she would use the tool of communication, negotiation and win-win agreements to get what he/she thinks he/she needs.

Emotions can be contagious. The emotions of one person may promote a similar emotion in another person, if they allow it. Sadness may elicit sadness, joy may promote joy, anger invite anger in return, or anxiety arouse anxiety. This is illustrated in the diagram opposite. The emotions of others can be overwhelming or leave us feeling battered, drained or dejected. However, others' feelings do not have to have this effect. Another's anger may bounce off us, when we are completely centred or in touch with our Essence. We may also render ourselves immune to the emotional assault of another by adopting a suitable perspective, which promotes a shift in our

A pictorial illustration of the various ways two different emotions may impact each other

The waves below represent the state of agitation. The narrower the waves, the higher the degree of agitation.

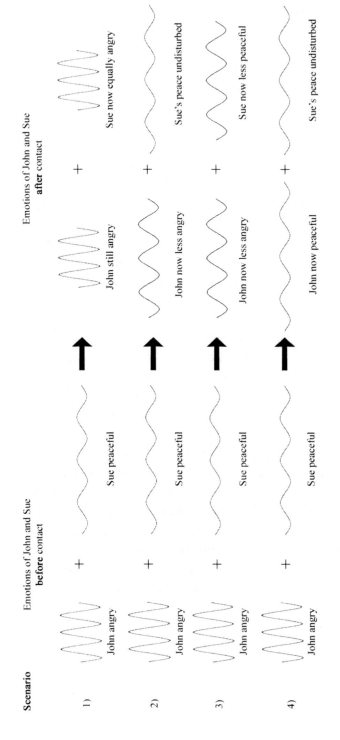

mood. Such a shift may be caused by focusing on the Essence of the other rather than the hurt Ego, which is lashing out, or by empathising with the pain of the other, which is crying out for help. Alternatively we may reside in a space where others' emotional turmoil simply flows right past us without ruffling a feather. We stay centred and calm in the face of others' raging upheavals. Maybe, in return, we have a calming effect on the emotions of the other.

We are responsible for the emotional charge that emanates from us and therefore we need to bear in mind the impact our emotions may have on the other. Equally, we are responsible for what we make of what we receive from others and how we act in response. Although 'airing' our feelings is preferential to suppressing or denying them, it is even more beneficial to us and others if we are able to experience our feelings in our own, private space. Yet it may be nonetheless appropriate and useful to let the other know what we are experiencing as a result of their comment, behaviour or attitude, especially if they are not aware of it and they are ready for feedback. However, when we do communicate our feelings, we need to do so once we have released the emotional charge and regained a calm, centred state. We also need to take ownership of our feelings and present them as something that is going on within us.

We are of great help to others if we are attuned to their sensitivities and issues. Whenever possible, we need to be careful to avoid being an instrument to reinforcing in others a less than helpful belief. However, on occasions acting as a trigger for somebody's 'negative' feelings is unavoidable, when doing otherwise would mean that we are denying our truth or betraying our integrity. It is always important to ascertain the meaning the other gives our communications and to endeavour to clarify our intention.

1.5 Possible responses when experiencing uncomfortable emotions

When we experience uncomfortable, unwelcome or painful emotions we may respond to them in a number of ways. Our responses may be grouped into two main categories. We may respond to the experience of unease, anger, frustration or any type of emotional pain either without an aware, reflective, deliberate intervention or in a consciously chosen, deliberate manner.

1. Responses not consciously or deliberately chosen

a) We react externally
We may see others as being responsible for how we feel. We retaliate by physically and/or verbally attacking the 'trigger' of our emotions. We accuse, blame, guilt-trip, label or judge and convict. We use our pain and the perceived offence against us as justification for committing all manner of assaults.

b) We react internally
Instead of lashing out externally we may respond to our negative experience of a particular situation by wrestling with the occurrence in our mind. Internally we seethe with anger or resentment or we grieve with disappointment. We mentally accuse or blame or berate the other(s) or ourselves.

c) We suppress or drown out our uncomfortable feelings
In response to our unease we may try to suppress or block out uncomfortable feelings by throwing ourselves into some activity such as work or entertainment or we deaden our feelings with alcohol or mind-altering drugs.

d) We unconsciously change our perspective

Instead of (as in a, b or c above) automatically maintaining or reinforcing an unhelpful perspective or creating a new detrimental viewpoint, resulting in feelings of unease or hurt, we may, without deliberate or conscious intention, change our mind. Somebody or something may draw our attention to an alternative, more beneficial perspective, which we may temporarily or even permanently adopt in place of the previously held viewpoint. This may occur temporarily, because the initially dominant perspective remains part of us, available to jump to the forefront on another occasion, or this may occur permanently, because the new perspective has such a powerful impact that the change of mind remains dominantly in place.

In any of the above responses, a) we do not realise that we have chosen a viewpoint or attitude and b) we are unaware of the content of our chosen perspective and thoughts or the character of our way of being. We also do not know that our uncomfortable feelings are due to the perspective we have chosen and not due to the outward occurrence. Equally, we do not recognise that the degree of unease of our feelings alerts us to the degree of discrepancy between our adopted viewpoint or notion and the one held at the Core of our Being. As we are not challenging the unhelpful adopted notion we keep it in place or if the same notion had already been chosen previously (and often it has been so many times before) we reinforce or strengthen this viewpoint. The viewpoint, now reinforced, will surface again, together with the feeling which that perspective arouses. However, the feelings will be somewhat stronger this time, because the notion has gained a greater momentum. The pattern of belief and experience continues.

2. Consciously and deliberately chosen responses

a) We consciously maintain our perspective

Once we become aware of a perspective or attitude which causes us to feel angry, frustrated, anxious or generally uneasy, we may not feel inclined to change our original stance. We hand over the reins to that part of us which champions the less than helpful stance. We succumb to the energy generated around this notion. Others may espouse the same opinion and thus augment the magnetism of that idea.

In this particular case, in contrast to the responses listed in point 1 above, we are aware of the issue, but we choose not to address it. We side with that part of us which is under the spell of the less beneficial perspective.

b) We interact with our emotions

Another consciously chosen response is to take our focus off the dramatic situation and to direct it onto our feelings. We acknowledge our emotions, perceive them and engage with them. We penetrate and experience them fully. This has a triple effect:

1) We no longer entertain the detrimental perspective, because our focus is elsewhere, that is on our feelings.
2) The focus on our feelings allows the accumulated energy to shift and even dissipate.
3) Often the attention to and interaction with our feelings yields some understanding or clarity with respect to the issue giving rise to the emotion.

c) We deliberately change our focus

In this type of response we purposefully remove our focus from the incident which triggered our uncomfortable feeling and we direct it elsewhere. We physically and mentally shift our focus and thus disengage the grip of the less than helpful stance. We no longer entertain the dysfunctional idea and thus we discontinue to strengthen the notion. In addition we halt the build-up of more negative emotional charge. However, we do not address the notion or belief and it remains part of our adopted viewpoint.

d) We deliberately change our perspective

In response to our uncomfortable feelings we may decide to change our viewpoint or attitude or way of being. This may occur in different ways:

o We may act according to a choice made beforehand. If we are already aware of particular issues, which surface repeatedly and result in certain habitual reactions, we may have determined on previous occasions the perspective we intend to switch to on such an occurrence.

o When our uncomfortable feelings make us aware that our stance or way of being is detrimental we may choose a different perspective from a pool of perspectives, which we have selected for such occasions. Such a pool of perspective may contain viewpoints such as:

What another person says is an indication of that person's world, where he/she is at. What I choose to do as a result of the communication is an indication of my world and who I choose to be *or*

Most likely we do not know completely the background from which the remark originated. Neither do we need to know. All we need to know is the perception or attitude we intend to adopt *or*

The person making a hurtful remark is him/herself embroiled in an issue *or*

If he/she knew better, he/she would act in a more beneficial way. Everybody wants to be happy. Inflicting pain on somebody else does not increase our feel-good factor. Therefore, nobody would choose to cause pain, if they were in possession of all the relevant data *or*

I get to choose the meaning here *or*

I am going to adopt the role of the creator here and I determine how I am going to experience this situation. I am going to be a host to my choice rather than a hostage to the other's choice. More examples are given in Part 3.

We may also choose a perspective which is presented by somebody or something there and then *or*

o We may adopt a different perspective out of a desire to do things differently or out of a decision to proactively switch to a more beneficial stance, when experiencing annoyance, frustration, disappointment or resentment amongst others.

In any of the above cases we deliberately change our thoughts or way of being in order to experience the situation now and in the future more beneficially.

e) We process our negative feelings
We deal with our uncomfortable feelings according to the process described in detail in Part 1.6. In using the process we consciously and deliberately make use of the brilliant opportunity presented by the onset of a negative emotion. We are clear that something is amiss with our perspective, attitude or way of being, when experiencing a negative emotion, and we fully appreciate that it would be beneficial to examine and take note of the message of our feelings. As part of the process we first disengage with the drama which has erupted within us and we pay attention to our feelings. Sometimes in perceiving and engaging with our feelings we become instantaneously clear which idea or perspective makes us so angry, frustrated or sad. Should we be unable to ascertain spontaneously what that viewpoint or notion is that is counterproductive to who we want to be, and out of touch with who we are in Essence, we have to probe more extensively. However, in order to do so productively, we have to be peaceful and centred and we have to proactively create a calm, uninterrupted space for ourselves. Such an exploration may be initiated with questions such as: 'Why is this comment or action so hurtful? What does this remark, interaction or behaviour represent to me? What do I say to myself when experiencing those feelings?' Some under-

standing or insight will emerge from such an enquiry. In some instances we may have to dig increasingly deeper in order to arrive at the root conviction or thought which is giving rise to our emotional pain. Once we have found the hurtful perspective we need to seek out and adopt a more helpful, good-feeling perspective. There is no limit as to how beneficial a perspective we adopt. The degree of elation that we feel will indicate how beneficial the perspective under consideration is.

Once we have adopted a more helpful alternative stance we have to readopt and revisit this viewpoint repeatedly in order to erode the original notion and to establish sufficiently the newly adopted perspective, attitude or way of being. We do so particularly when our feelings alert us that we have slipped back into our outdated, unhelpful thoughts.

f) We get in touch with or access our Core Self

This response is only available to us if we are quite adept in directly and closely connecting with our Essence (how this is done is shown in Part 3). If we are able to access our Intrinsic Self in the midst of negative emotions, we immediately switch to a positive emotion and instantaneously experience a shift in our perspective. In successfully seeking the realm of our Core Self we withdraw by default from the unhelpful viewpoint or issue and automatically join the beneficial perspective of our Essence. The additional advantage of connecting with our Authentic Self is that on each occasion we employ this method we weaken the unhelpful perspective and boost our Core way of being.

To what degree some of the above options are available to us depends on how strongly we are in the grip of a negative emotion and under the spell of a dysfunctional belief and to what extend we are adept in changing our perception or perspective. When we are fully immersed and at the centre of a whirlpool of a strong emotional current and part of us is strongly attached to the unhelpful belief, it is much more difficult to step back and disengage the detrimental idea, and a more powerful intervention is required. We may have to physically remove ourselves from the triggering situation or environment or we have to powerfully, with determination, focus on a different activity or thought. Therefore it is useful to be alert and sensitive to the onset of a negative emotion, while it is still relatively easy to change our mind.

Removing our focus from the trigger is not the same as avoiding our feelings. It is simply a decision not to deal with our feelings there and then. We may at any time reactivate our feelings by mentally revisiting the trigger (we do this by recalling or thinking about the event again) and then following the process as described below.

If we are not able to access our Essence directly, then we receive the greatest benefit from our uncomfortable feelings by processing our emotions as described in section e. As part of the process our feelings shift, the build-up of emotional energy dissipates, we discover a notion or attitude which in many ways impedes us, and we repeatedly replace the detrimental viewpoint with a more beneficial one until this more helpful perspective is fully established and integrated. This method represents one of the fastest way of discovering and eroding a dysfunctional belief and reaping all the benefit this entails. So let's look at the process in more detail.

1.6 The process of making beneficial use of our uncomfortable emotions

The following is a description of the process that I recommend when experiencing negative emotions. The process may initially appear somewhat lengthy. However, with practise and experience, the process may at times be finished within seconds or minutes. At other times, especially in the early stages, it may require a certain amount of probing and deliberating.

1. Noticing and acknowledging our emotions

In order to process our uncomfortable feelings we have to first of all become aware of our feelings. Feelings may range from extremely painful, excruciating sensations to mild fluctuations in our body energy. It is usually pretty easy to notice strong emotions, but even then feelings may be denied or blocked out. With more subtle feelings it may take acute awareness to perceive them. In order to become aware of any slight feelings we may have to become more attuned to our body sensations and energy fluctuations. By carefully and regularly paying attention to our body sensations, we sensitise ourselves to our feelings, until eventually we notice every hint of emotion.

The process under discussion starts with recognising and accepting that we are experiencing a particular emotion. There are many reasons why we might ignore or deny our feelings. Here are some of them:

o We may fear that our emotions might embarrass us, disadvantage us or meet the disapproval of others. However, we do not have to display our feelings. We only have to acknowledge them to ourselves, pay attention to and own them in order to benefit from them.

o We may judge our feelings negatively, consider them as uncaring, self-centred or repulsive or perceive them as unprofessional or as a sign of weakness or immaturity.
o We may fear that our feelings might get out of control.

Even if we find some of our negative feelings such as rage, jealousy or embarrassment inconvenient and troublesome, it would serve us well to receive them with open arms. They are important and valuable messengers and the more we value them, the more we can gain from them.

2. Taking ownership of our emotions

This is an absolutely decisive step. In order to reap the benefit of any negative emotion and in order to uncover and change the unhelpful notion which is giving rise to it, we have to accept the premise that it is our thoughts which produce our feelings. We create our feelings when we choose a particular perspective or attitude with respect to an incident. When we give the happening a meaning we also choose how we are going to feel. Yet in cases where we choose our perspective and thus our feelings unconsciously, our emotions may appear involuntary or caused by another.

However, in failing to take ownership of our feelings:

o We place someone or something in charge of our experience; we see ourselves powerless and dependent on others for a satisfactory outcome.
o We forsake the opportunity to let go of something which affects us negatively.
o We forgo a chance to grow in understanding and wisdom.

Thus owning our feelings is crucial. Therefore I remind myself regularly 'I own all my experiences'. I do so particularly when I am in a situation I would rather not be in. It is so easy to slip back into blaming others, when we have practised it for as long as I have. It can be very tempting to adopt the victim role and self-righteously feel justified to convict and punish the 'perceived perpetrator'. This is not to negate that some overt response or outward action may eventually be appropriate or recommended. However, irrespective of any outer action, any uncomfortable feeling indicates that something in our perspective or attitude is counterproductive and it is worthwhile addressing this. Therefore, ownership of our negative emotions is a crucial step in moving past the repetition of a particular type of experience. Doing so also brings about an immediate shift in the way we feel.

3. Experiencing our emotions

Besides acknowledging and owning our emotions we need to pay attention to them; we need to perceive and 'hear' them. In order to do so we have to take our attention off the incident or anything else and direct it onto the sensations in our body and the turmoil in our mind. We have to exclusively and attentively notice, stay with and feel the sensations, which may be nausea in the stomach, a pounding heart, a change in our breathing, a numbing in our limbs, increased pulse rate, a tightening of the chest, a tensing of various muscles, a furrowing of the brow, a clenching of fists, feeling cold or hot, increased turbulence in the mind, a flow of tears, a desire to scream or hit out or run away. Less dramatic feelings manifest as more subtle sensations such as slight changes in our body energy or changes in our sense of ease, aliveness or level of joy.

When a particular feeling becomes too intense and powerful for us to stay with it, we can always bring ourselves out of the flow of the emotion by focusing on our breath or on our surroundings. We can then re-activate that feeling again, maybe in a toned-down version, when we feel strong enough.

When we focus on our emotions with full attention, they will move through various phases, run their course and eventually dissipate. That means the presently built-up emotional energy has been exhausted.

We may experience our feelings as soon as they are triggered or it may be advisable to take ourselves away from the situation if our feelings are too powerful to handle there and then. We may always 'shelve' a feeling, if that is more appropriate, and re-activate it again in a quiet, private moment by mentally revisiting the triggering scenario.

It is advisable to 'hear' or experience our feelings for at least three reasons:

o When our emotions go unnoticed, they remain part of the accumulation of energy around a particular idea.
o When we pay attention to our feelings, we shift our focus from the triggering, unhelpful viewpoint and we no longer strengthen that particular viewpoint.
o Often our attention to and interaction with our feelings affords us some insight into the nature of the perspective or way of being which causes them.

As just mentioned, experiencing and releasing our feelings sometimes affords us immediately some insights or understanding of what underlying idea gave rise to the emotion, and that might be all that is needed. At other times the underlying assumptions and beliefs may be less obvious and we may have to do some exploration.

4. Exploring the underlying cause of our emotions

In order to access the notion or perspective which set our feelings in motion we have to:

o Seek out (the sooner the better) some quiet, uninterrupted time and location and make it a high priority to create an undisturbed time for ourselves.
o Show great courage and honesty in order to confront and

own what we may have long evaded or disowned, because
we judge it negatively.

o Be emotionally in a calm, peaceful and focused space, with
  our mind being relatively still and free from distraction.
  Some calming, centring exercise may be necessary. Focusing
  and following our breath may effectively facilitate this.
  Other methods such as going for a walk, doing some
  physical exercise, listening to peaceful music or writing our
  thoughts down may also be effective. We need to experiment
  and find what works for us.

Once we have created a suitable environment and conditions,
we need to remind ourselves of the triggering scenario and the
feelings we felt and then start the exploration with a series of
questions. Here are some of the initial questions we might ask
ourselves in order to get closer to what is the cause of our hurt
or discomfort:

> What specifically am I reacting to?
> What really gets to me here?
> Why do I find this behaviour, comment or interaction so
> offensive or hurtful?
> What thoughts come up when experiencing this emotion?
> What is the notion, the image, the quality or the sentiment
> that is stirring those feelings?
> What does this action, response, behaviour, situation
> represent or symbolise to me?
> What meaning do I give it? How do I interpret this?
> How would I classify or label this interaction, statement or
> behaviour? For example would I label it as judging me, as
> not accepting me, as ridicule, as not respecting me, as
> deceitful, as a betrayal, as feeling incompetent, worthless?
> What do I say to myself here?
> What do I seek that I am not getting?
> What am I not getting that I think I need?

Only a few of the questions may be relevant to the particular investigation at hand. We need to listen carefully to what thoughts or hunches emerge in our awareness when we ask ourselves some of the above questions. What words come to mind? What do we hear ourselves saying? What realisations begin to dawn?

The first set of questions may only guide us to the uppermost idea which causes us discomfort. Often ideas or beliefs come in clusters with one notion associated with another thought, which in turn is linked to a further, more basic sentiment. Our ideas or beliefs are grouped like the layers of an onion around a core belief. A core belief is one of our most basic, fundamental beliefs and it is generally the most decisive, influential and often most pernicious belief in the chain of our enquiry and thus the most highly charged. The more intensely unpleasant an emotion is, the more limiting, retarding or detrimental is the perspective or notion giving rise to it. Core beliefs are usually most deeply buried in our subconscious. Yet it is extremely worthwhile to come across a core belief, because our core beliefs exert the greatest unconscious influence on our choices of perspective, attitudes and behaviour. For me some of the core beliefs I discovered as part of my enquiries were the notions that I am not being accepted, am not worthwhile, am not being heard or seen, am incompetent, am being misjudged and am not being cared for or supported.

If in our exploration the intensity and magnitude of our feelings appear to be out of proportion with the notion yielded by our initial enquiry, then we need to dig deeper. After further probing as to why the so far discovered notion is so painful, we will find an underlying, more painful idea. If we continue to ask ourselves why the second idea is so hurtful, we may discover an even more critical thought or belief. Our intuition or sense of 'rightness' will guide us as to whether we have reached the central idea. For me I usually had a strong, clear sense of 'this is it', 'this is why my friend's remark hurt me so much'. When we have uncovered the most basic, most critical belief, we have a profound 'aha' moment. Our mood and thoughts shift. I always experienced a great relief, excitement and exhilaration and immense gratefulness for my increased understanding.

As part of my own explorations, which gave rise to this book, I found it particularly astounding and staggering that my most painful core issues such as my craving for being accepted by significant others, was something that I was not doing myself. I was not accepting myself to a large extent and yet I expected others to accept me where I would not. Of course, I was not at all aware that lack of acceptance of myself and others was an issue for me. All I knew was that X made a very hurtful remark and he/she behaved abominably. Only when I looked more deeply into what was going on did I become aware of the under-lying issue and only much later still did I discover that the underlying issue had to do with what I was doing or thinking. For example I was not paying attention to my Inner Self or Intrinsic Being and yet I expected others to pay attention to me. I was misjudging, labelling, not valuing or appreciating myself and others, but I perceived others as treating me in this manner and I reacted with disappointment, indignation and hurt. I thought those close to me were not taking responsibility for themselves. On investigation I realised, that

    a. I was taking inappropriate responsibility for others *and*
    b. I was not taking full responsibility for what was in my world. There were times when I felt the victim and resorted to blaming others. There were situations and occurrences which I did not own or accept as my creation.

When I realised all of this the process became extremely inter-esting and exciting to me. Time and time again processing my pain, anger, frustration or disappointment brought me back to myself and highlighted something that I was doing or not doing and which I objected to in others.

How this stage is carried out in practice is illustrated with specific examples in the next chapter. You will see from those descriptions that one bout of emotional turmoil may bring up a whole range of realisations and insights. Also many different incidents may bring us back to the same core issues for us to work with them some more.

The crucial aspect of this step is to bring our perspectives and beliefs to our conscious awareness so that we can make informed choices. Why we have adopted a particular notion is not important. What is important is what we are doing about it, now that we have become aware of it.

5. Making conscious, deliberate choices with regard to what we have discovered

Now that we have found the root of our uncomfortable emotion some choices have to be made and the more deliberately we make those choices the more consciously and intentionally we decide our future experiences. In order to productively and beneficially process our negative feelings, some helpful changes are necessary.

When we have uncovered a perspective, idea or belief which is not in line with our highest aspirations or who we want to be, it is time to let go of this notion and adopt a more empowering, advantageous one. To find the most beneficial perspective may require a certain degree of deliberation and experimentation. There are a limitless number of improved perspectives available out there, all of which would create a more pleasant experience for us. A small selection of beneficial notions are given in Part 3 under the heading of 'shifters' and some more can be found in the next chapter and elsewhere. If we have the sincere intention to find an improved idea, we will do so without fail. If a suitable, better-feeling idea does not present itself spontaneously, a good place to start is by exploring what idea would create the experience we desire. We may ask ourselves: 'How do I want to be and what idea is compatible with that?' or 'What do I want to achieve or have in my life and what thought or notion complies with that?'

We need to play around with different thoughts or ideas and use our feelings to gauge the degree of improvement. Our body sensations of comfort or discomfort, enthusiasm or reluctance, will lead us to the most beneficial and elevating perspective or sentiment.

Once we have found the most elating idea we have to firmly commit to it, particularly when the old, out-dated idea has gathered a great momentum. In comparison, the newly adopted idea is frequently weak and minute. Therefore, it often needs to be nurtured and reinforced to the nth degree to firmly establish the preferred notion and to sufficiently erode the old idea. This is illustrated in the next step.

If we have become aware that previously unbeknown to us we exhibit a certain quality, attitude or way of being e.g. being untruthful, unreliable, close-minded, aggressive, manipulative, which we want to change, we have to first acknowledge and accept this quality. We can only change what we make our own. Then we have to become clear which quality, attitude or way of being we would rather promote instead. Then we have to commit fully to our choice and deliberate what needs to be in place in order to lovingly and persistently nurture and cultivate the desired quality.

The exploration stage may have made us aware of a need, or passion, or dream which was not on our 'to do' list, but which is important to take seriously for our overall well-being. In such a case we have several options such as:

o We may make those concerned aware of our needs, desire or passion. For example, if we want to be supported in a particular area or in a particular way, then we need to communicate this clearly. This needs to be done from a relaxed, peaceful place and fully owning our needs as ours, without making others responsible for them.

o We may give ourselves what we seek from others. For example, if we crave acceptance from those close to us, we instead strive to accept ourselves as we are right now, with all our imagined imperfections. If we do not want to be judged, then we need to stop judging ourselves and others. If we want to be supported, we need to support ourselves to whatever extent necessary. If we perceive a need or passion for a particular creative expression, then we need to explore avenues and undertake steps to do so. We have to make this a high priority and elicit all the help we can get.

o We may transcend the need altogether. Moving past a need is not to be confused with denying that we have a need. It just means we have moved to a place where the need no longer exists. Getting to this place is a gradual process and cannot be forced. A very effective and fast way to transcend a need is to give others what we think we crave for ourselves. Eventually, of its own accord, it no longer matters whether, e.g., we are accepted or not. Either way we are perfectly at ease and satisfied with the level of acceptance or non-acceptance by any significant other.

When we have discovered a previously unrecognised behavioural pattern and we find that it is not in line with who we want to be, we have to search for and choose a new, more beneficial way of operating to take the place of the old habit.

The decision step may also include a decision to undertake a particular outward action or communication. It may be helpful to let the other(s) know what effect a particular action had on us, particularly if the other is open to feedback. However, this step needs to be undertaken whilst we are in a peaceful, centred state and from a position of good-will; we need to become first clear:

> Will this action or communication improve anything?
> Is it instrumental in promoting beneficial changes?

The action has to be undertaken with the intention of bringing about positive changes for us and others and **not** with the intention of 'getting even' or 'balancing out' a hurt with another hurt. Inflicting pain does not diminish the first pain; it only adds to the initial pain. The only way to diminish hurt is by letting go and changing our mind.

6. Making the changes

This step is extremely important and not to be underestimated in terms of what is required. Having unconsciously programmed ourselves one way we now have to purposefully programme ourselves according to our newly chosen maxim. The reprogramming may occur relatively easy. On the other hand it may require considerable input and effort. We may have automatically opted for the same perspective or judgement millions of times and the old way of operating or thinking may have gained a powerful momentum. It may have become deeply embedded in our mental structure and will exert a powerful influence over our automatic choices. We must not underestimate how persistent and influential some ideas and beliefs can be. In general, the greater the momentum and power that a particular habit or idea has acquired, the more energy and input are required to bring about the change. We have to generate a sufficient amount of impetus to bring an old idea to a halt and to get a new idea or pattern off the ground.

Thus the change will require input to a varying degree by way of:

o A compelling motivation, commitment, resolve and determination. Our motivation may have to be powerful enough to halt and reshape a long-established pattern. The change has to be made a high enough priority in order to make it happen.

   It might be useful to build up some leverage, something which makes the need for change so desirable and compelling, that an alternative action or notion is not an option. This will vary from person to person and we each know best what thought or action will have this effect. Also, some kind of strategy needs to be in place which serves to reinforce and keep virile the intention and commitment. For example this may take the form of notes displayed in prominent places, or a daily routine which involves revisiting a set of reminders e.g. first thing in the morning or last thing at night. We have to be creative and experiment to find the most suitable method for us. We need all the help and reminders we can organise.

o Inspiring ourselves, firing up our enthusiasm, arousing our passion and thus boosting the energy driving the change. A pep-talk with ourselves might help. We need to become our own coach and our most fervent supporter.

o Enlisting all the resources we can, for example in the form of supportive others such as friends or colleagues. Anything that nurtures and elevates our spirit is highly recommended.

o Being creative, inventive and playful to ferret out the most effective method.

o Being vigilant and alert. This is also quite important. Our old ways of operating are so familiar and strongly habitual that they effortlessly creep back unnoticed and easily escape our attention. Yet fortunately we have the assistance of our emotions to alert us that we are indulging an outdated notion and pattern.

o Definitely being relentlessly persistent until the goal of change is achieved. Stringent discipline may have to be employed to effect some of the changes successfully.

o Being patient with the process and with those aspects of ours which resist the change. The change may involve doing something we lack confidence in. We may feel embarrassed or vulnerable or open to ridicule or we may fear failure. Some part of us may be anxious and defensive about leaving a very familiar and crucial idea behind and replacing it with an unfamiliar, alien concept or notion. It is helpful to refrain from judging the outdated idea negatively and to reassure ourselves of the considerable benefits of the new idea. We need to address any arising difficulty and be patient, compassionate with and accepting of all our aspects. Yet we have to remain firm and persistent and not allow ourselves to be diverted from pursuing the intended change. The change will occur of its own accord, in its own timing, if all the above-mentioned is in place and we reinforce out initial decision each time we are confronted with the issue.

Some or all of the above may be necessary to starve or erode a deep-seated, powerful belief and for the favoured new belief to become anchored into our mental web so that the new perspective becomes our default response. In order for this to happen, every time a negative emotion makes us aware that an old belief has surfaced again, we need to withdraw our focus from the non-beneficial perspective, idea, attitude or need, and immediately refocus our attention onto the preferred new perspective or practise our new behaviour or way of being. We may affirm: 'I don't do this anymore. I am ... now.' Or 'I believe ... now.' Seemingly endless repetition may be necessary before the new idea or behaviour is fully integrated at all levels. It can also happen instantaneously.

Many factors may challenge our wish and intention to do the 'work' and to move past inhibiting, undesired experiences and happenings. Some of these are:

o Change can seem unsettling and threatening
   a) to some of our aspects as mentioned above *and*
   b) to others, especially those close to us e.g. family or friends, who have a vested interest in us not upseting the status quo and thus they may bring pressure to bear.
o Not fully appreciating the rationale for doing the process, the implications of not processing our negative feelings or what is achieved and gained from the 'work'.
o A part of us sabotaging our intention with the idea that we cannot do it or persuading ourselves not to do all that is necessary or not supporting ourselves in what promotes the change.

Once we have applied the process a few times we become more adept in the use of it; understanding and clarity emerge faster and the emotions abate quicker. In addition, when we have come across a certain issue repeatedly, we start to become quite alert to particular aspects of the issue and we recognise more quickly when we are under the spell of that issue. This allows us to extricate ourselves from the spell more easily and to place an aspect of our choice in the driver's seat. For example through years of acting out the victim I am quite familiar with the characteristics of that way of being and I easily spot when I have slipped back into that role.

Advantages of processing our uncomfortable feelings as just described:

o We make use of a brilliant opportunity to become aware of and transform unhelpful perspectives, convictions, habits or needs.
o Using our strong negative feelings as described above leads us to what is most important for us to address and modify.
o We may use the process to open our eyes as to how we cause ourselves pain, how we give ourselves a hard time, how we get in our own way and how we prevent ourselves from having and experiencing what we yearn for.
o The process a) releases buried emotions, which, even in their dormant state are part of our Being and invariably influence our overall well-being negatively, and b) allows us to exit the cycle of creating the same unwelcome experiences.
o The process is an extremely powerful avenue for gaining insights, increased awareness, greater clarity and under-standing, increased freedom and peace. It represents one of the tools which facilitates the alignment with our Essence or Core Self.

Processing my emotions has completely changed my experience of life. Previously I experienced my existence as an immense struggle. I felt victimised, I experienced a roller-coaster of emotions such as immense anger, resentment, frustration, restlessness, anxiety, being at the mercy of those close to me, allowing myself to be manipulated to the nth degree and manip-ulating skilfully in return, feeling deeply misunderstood, misjudged, betrayed, not being accepted by those whose accept-ance I craved, feeling totally incompetent, inadequate and above all unworthy. Even my first class Honours Degree and

PhD only superficially masked the roots of judging myself inadequate and worthless. Because I had acquired such monumental, deep-seated issues and because I only discovered and developed the process en route, it took an enormous amount of repetition and considerable time to transform those issues and change my mind. Yet, because I had unconsciously chosen such limiting, retarding, pernicious beliefs, which I perpetuated (of course unconsciously) so fervently and obstinately, the results of taking advantage of my feelings and changing my mind were the more substantial, magnificent and worthwhile. Processing my feelings and changing my mind has brought me from experiencing immense limitations, dissatisfaction and powerlessness to a life of deep peace, ease, inner security, of greatly increased clarity and understanding, of experiencing huge elevation and lightness, and above all immensely increased, breathtaking inner power and freedom.

1.7 How I used the process

I have processed my feelings in the above manner for more than 20 years and I have come across and worked with a huge number of issues. Most of them are in the distant past and forgotten. However, there are a few instances I can still remember, which I refer to here in order to demonstrate what the process may look like in practice and to illustrate some of the scope of the process.

Example 1
Carefully and tentatively I manoeuvred my brand-new car out of the garage, which was barely wide enough to house the car. There was a slight resistance and a scraping sound. After some correction, I finally extricated the car from the garage. On inspection, to my utmost horror, I found a dent on the off-side wing. This dent exploded out of proportion in my mind. A whole range of emotions boiled up inside of me. Physically I felt nauseous and I trembled slightly. My breathing became shallow and my heart raced. I felt hot and cold at the same time. Great anger welled up and an avalanche of thoughts raced through my mind. 'This is the last thing I need. The car is less than two weeks old. X will absolutely hit the roof.' I thought of all the criticism and barrage of blame that I expected to descend on me. Worse than that, he will feel proven 'right' in his assumption that I am careless and prone to cause damage. This was the strongest trigger for my anger, disappointment and underlying deep hurt. This hurt so deeply that it almost manifested as physical pain in the heart area.

My feelings being so intense and powerful, something I had not experienced for a long, long time, made it initially difficult for me to take a step back. I was already late for driving my children to school and myself to work and I felt quite short-tempered and stressed. However, I did manage to take hold of my tools and put them into practice. I refrained from acting out my feelings and resisted my impulse to direct my anger against my two children, who were slow getting ready for school. Then I reminded myself to refrain from self-recrimination and that this was not about the dent in the car, but about some under-lying reason and that I could gain greatly here. My anger subsided almost immediately, but my hurt stayed with me in the background for most of my working day.

When I eventually had some time to myself, I took myself back to the incident and reactivated the full force of my emotions. At the thought of the scratch I felt sick in the stomach and extremely disappointed and furious with myself. A whole range of other feelings rose up, made themselves felt and then subsided and disappeared, until eventually only an underlying deep sadness and intense despair lingered. I wanted to be swallowed up and disappear.

Once I had stayed with those sentiments for a while and they had eased off, I started to explore the underlying issues. I asked myself 'Which notion caused those powerful feelings? What does this incident mean to me?'

This is what I became aware of:

o My issue around competence had become active again; traces of my once deeply held, unconscious belief that I am incompetent, clumsy and careless had come to the fore-front.

o In addition my monumental core belief that I am not worth-while had surfaced once more and set in motion a powerful emotional force. I had come across this issue many times before and each time worked to replace this self-defeating notion. Therefore, I was surprised at the power and influence it still exerted. Deep down some part of me still believed strongly that I am not deserving, even that I do not deserve to exist.

○ I also became aware of my compulsion for perfection.
○ My all-prevailing, monumental issue around not being accepted was once again confronting me.
○ Some of what I had dished out in the past was coming home to roost.

As a result of those realisations and insights I decided:

○ To step up and work on accepting myself and others to a higher degree.
○ To be more aware of the level of acceptance that I already enjoy and to focus less on incidents of perceived non-acceptance.
○ To pay more attention to my compulsion for perfection and to let it go.
○ To consciously affirm to myself that I do deserve this beautiful car and own my decision to get it.
○ To seek, with a higher priority and commitment, to get more deeply in touch with my Essence i.e. that part of me where I am infinitely worthwhile and my worth is never in doubt.
○ To take another conscious step in letting go of my deeply held belief that I am inept and to reinforce the idea that I am able and skilled.

After the initial shock and flurry of other emotions, I knew I could gain greatly from this event, however much I initially wished it away. It is important to stress here that the same incident would have affected someone else quite differently, especially someone who did not have those issues. Yet it produced for me, despite its seeming 'unpleasantness', a whole range of extremely helpful insights and afforded me the opportunity to release further my deep sense of worthlessness.

Example 2
After I declined the request to attend a special social event I was accused, yet again, of delighting in being different. It was said that it was a compulsion of mine. I was labelled as odd and peculiar. This has always been a source of huge pain, anger and sadness for me. This is what I did:

o I acknowledged that the remark hurt me; I perceived my indignation, my sense of being wronged, being misjudged and being treated unfairly. I allowed myself to experience the surge of anger, pain and sadness.

o I reminded myself that the pain was generated by what I made of the comments. The unpleasant feelings were due to the fact that the meanings I had given those statements were out of step with the perspective of the Core of my Being.

Then I started my exploration around the underlying issues of the pain:

Question: Why does it hurt me to be labelled this way?
Answer: It means to me that I am not recognised. It means to me that I am not accepted.

I felt a huge pain around not being recognised or accepted.

Question: Why is not being accepted and not being recognised so immensely painful to me?
Answer: After staying with this question for a while it occurred to me, like a flash of lightning, that it was actually I who did not accept me. I rejected many aspects of myself and judged myself harshly.

The extent to which I criticised and berated myself was a huge surprise to me. I was totally unaware how un-accepting of myself I was. In addition I was quite oblivious of my innate qualities such as my strength, my capacity for love and wisdom. By the way, I believe everybody has these qualities at the Core of their Being.

I also realised that I was not as accepting of others as I thought I was. This was a huge eye-opener for me, because I prided myself in being accepting and non-judgemental (I did not discriminate on the basis of race, religion, gender, social standing). However, on closer examination I had to confront the fact that I was prejudiced against people when they did not deal with their problems and move on. This prejudice resulted from my difficulty at seeing people suffer. I always felt responsible for others and a strong need to eliminate suffering and limitations. Now I am able to allow others to choose suffering, albeit still feeling some sadness about their choice. This acceptance of their choice exists within me alongside my immense passion for people to achieve greater freedom and empowerment. However, back then the perceived suffering of others fuelled my prejudice and non-acceptance of them.

In light of this I resolved to do my utmost to accept fully all the choices that others make. This was a huge decision, made repeatedly since then, and I am still working on this. In addition I resolved to strive to accept myself fully, all aspects of myself, the good, the bad and the ugly, and to appreciate my innate qualities.

In the subsequent weeks and months many interactions occurred which revealed, on investigation, a core pain around the issue of not being accepted. In time I realised how much I grieved about not having received acceptance, about not being recognised, understood, truly known. An all-consuming sadness, pain and mourning enveloped me at times. Staying with the rawness and soreness of my hurt and the monumental pain, the emotions finally exhausted themselves and disappeared. Each time I resolved not to hold on to the sense of being wronged, misjudged or treated unfairly. In addition, on each occasion I renewed and reinforced my commitment to accept myself and others more fully. Because this was such a huge, deeply embedded issue for me, it took a strong commitment and endless repetition to change the habit of judging myself 'negatively' and to work on my sense of self-worth.

Example 3

One particular type of occurrence in my partner relationship caused great frustration, annoyance and hurt. Most attempts to convey my views and preferences were met with immediate dismissal and angry rejection. My opinions and my choices were labelled as a compulsion to be different or as games I play. This meant to me, albeit yet unconsciously, that my choices, beliefs or views could not be taken seriously or did not matter and more deeply unconsciously I harboured the idea that I did not matter. Initially I handled this by keeping my opinions and beliefs to myself and by subconsciously grieving about being apparently of so little consequence.

This issue of mine in turn, as often is the case, dovetailed perfectly with one of my partner's issues. My partner found it quite difficult to hear my likes and dislikes and opinions because he saw my difference in taste and views as a rejection of him. Of course I did not realise that at the time. All I knew then was that, yet again, somebody did not accept me, somebody found aspects of me unsettling and threatening, and yet again, they refused to get to know me.

Once I had started to ask questions instead of adopting the victim role, I made the connection that in childhood I had the same experiences of non-acceptance and disinterest, of being seen as odd and feeling invisible. Perceiving myself as invisible hurt immensely. It brought a whole range of sensations from outrage to deep sadness, despair and intense longing and a sense of loss. Sensing my feelings brought a sense of relief, lightness and expanse.

On further exploration I realised how crucial it was to me to be seen and understood. Suddenly it occurred to me that this was something I had to address within myself. I did not understand and see myself and it was vital for me to discover and understand myself to a much greater extent. Actually, on the last occasion this issue arose I shouted, out of the blue, 'You are not interested in getting to know me!' That was for me the most powerful, emphatic hint that it is high time for me to get to know me. By the way, since then I have noticed on many occasions how informative and revealing it can be to listen to what we are saying to others and to ourselves. We often send powerful messages to ourselves as part of our remarks to others. Likewise, sometimes something in what others communicate jumps out at us, trying to get our attention and to alert us to something important.

As a result of the understanding I gained I decided to make it a high priority to get to know myself more comprehensively. In addition, I determined to be more cognisant of the degree to which I am already seen and recognised. I also determined to listen more acutely to the underlying message of what somebody has to say and to give feedback of what I have received.

Example 4

On many occasions I had reacted sensitively when phone calls were not returned, or when I was not contacted as promised, or others never took the initiative to get in touch.

Here is an example of the exploration I conducted after I felt hurt, angry and resentful, when Kim (as I call her here) did not come as arranged and did not let me know that she was not coming. After realising that there was an issue at play, and not allowing myself to fall back into the victim role, I made time for an exploration, which went something like this:

> *Question:* Why am I upset about this? Irrespective of the fact that this could be seen as inconsiderate, what specifically upsets me here?
>
> *Answer:* It means to me that I am not important to her, that she does not really care about me.
>
> *Question:* Why does her apparent not caring hurt me?
>
> *Answer:* Pain around this had come up for me many times before. It touched on my childhood experience, when I so wanted to be cared for instead of doing the caring. As a result I had adopted the belief that I am not worth other people's time. Many incidents played out this belief and confirmed it repeatedly in line with my expectations.

I worked with this as follows:

○ I adopted the stance that I had chosen this particular interpretation with respect to the above incident. Kim's behaviour could have been interpreted in any number of ways. Maybe Kim was rather disorganised that day. Her action was not directed against me. She, like everybody else, did what she knew how to. What I do as a result is my choice and responsibility.

○ I appreciated that this was another incident to confront me with the deeply held belief that I am not worth other people's time or more poignantly that I am not worthwhile.

o I allowed myself to let go some more of the pain in this area and to boost my sense of self-worth.

o Then I asked myself: 'Do I care for myself?'

I realised that I do not give enough attention to my Core Self and that I neglect to some extent the needs of my body. As a result I resolved to pay more attention to the whispers of my Essence and to improve my time- and energy-management and not to pander to the Ego of others at the cost of myself. I also decided to be more considerate of my body needs, especially with respect to what I eat.

Example 5

A close relative of mine, here called Jasmine, accused me of being weak because I showed my emotions within a small family gathering. As a result I felt indignant, angry and deeply hurt. Refraining from retaliating verbally and realising that something powerful had been triggered, I proceeded with my exploration at the first undisturbed moment:

Question: Why was I reacting so strongly? What meaning triggered the reaction?

Answer: I felt misjudged and unrecognised.

Question: Why is this so upsetting for me?

Realisation: My monumental issue around not being truly seen has been activated again.

Question: 'Do I recognise others?'

Answer: Searching honestly I had to admit that at times I am not open to 'seeing' others. There are occasions when I pigeon-hole people I meet and thus limit myself from seeing all there is to see. I am not open to the full spectrum of their personality, if my assumptions limit my 'view' of them.

Decision: To do my utmost to refrain from labelling or judging.

Question: 'Do I recognise myself?'

Answer: Reluctantly I had to admit that I was still judging myself harshly in all manner of ways and yet I expected others to recognise and value me. As a consequence I determined to refrain from judging myself. In addition I resolved to let go of my requirement of others to see me and to appreciate more the extent to which I am already valued and recognised.

Although I made this decision back then, I can see now that the need to be recognised by others would have automatically lessened and disappeared once I had learned to recognise myself. However, I think the Ego will always be flattered by recognition.

I have never told Jasmine what emotional turmoil her remark triggered. It would not have served any purpose. For one, she was, and still is, convinced that she judged me correctly. Secondly, she is not in a place to hear or make use of what I have to say. Thirdly, the incident occurred to show me **my** issues and was there for **my** benefit.

I also realised that making Jasmine responsible for my feelings would entail making my peace and happiness dependent on what she says, does or thinks. This I considered to be uncaring and unloving to Jasmine and to myself, because it does not cater for either of us to be in charge of our life. Instead I learned to appreciate that I can gain greatly from my feelings.

Example 6
I had interpreted several remarks of my partner as indicating that I am incompetent and inept.
  Looking into this, two realisations emerged:
  1. The realisation that somewhere within me I considered myself inept. I had been in denial of this aspect of myself, because I so wanted to be competent. Therefore I ignored that part of me that believed otherwise. On a conscious level I sided with that part of me that saw myself as competent and able. It took years of instances and much pain to confront myself with the part that I so obstinately tried to deny.
    However, acknowledging this notion and confronting this part, being with it and hearing it, changed that part.

ecame my 'ally' instead of being my undercover
ny'. As a consequence I was a great deal freer to be
...o I wanted to be.

2. I asked myself 'Why did I so desperately want to be
competent?'
Realisation: If I were incompetent, I would be worthless.

My deeply unconscious, obstinately held notion that I am
worthless had surfaced again.

Question: What is the problem with being worthless?
Answer: Being worthless means I do not deserve to exist.
This realisation brought up a nauseating sensation in the
pit of my stomach. I also experienced deep sadness,
despair, depression and grieving. I experienced and
released my feelings and affirmed, with great intention and
conviction, my indisputable, innate worth.

Example 7
Once a pupil of mine suggested that I was not a good teacher. I
reacted strongly to this and felt dejected, hurt and depressed.
My examination of the underlying issues went as follows:

Question: X gives me a view of her world. Why am I
offended and hurt by it?
Answer: Because, as I already know, I react strongly to the
notion that I am inept. For me incompetence is associated
with the notion that I do not have the 'right' to express
myself. As a child I 'learnt' that to 'express' myself results
in trouble and pain. I also realised that the incident had
touched on some of the remaining pain around not being
'heard' or 'seen', which had been identified in many explorations before.

After letting go some more of the pain, I resolved, with strong
intention:

o To 'hear' and pay close attention to my Authentic Self *and*
o To aim to get to a point where everybody I come across, is
'heard' and receives my undivided attention. Albeit a grand

task for me, it is certainly something I can work towards.

o   To affirm myself as competent and worthwhile.
o   To seek out ways of 'expressing' myself to a greater extent.

I was very moved by those realisations and felt deep gratitude towards that particular pupil.

Example 8

On several occasions I experienced enormous pain along with intense anger, indignation, grieving and a feeling of loss around incidents of betrayal. People who I trusted, valued and thought highly of and who in turn, so I thought, appreciated me, expressed their low opinion of me to others in my absence. On each occasion, this caused great emotional turmoil.

After experiencing and releasing my feelings, I examined the underlying issues.

> *Question:* Why is betrayal by someone I trusted so hurtful?
> *Answer:* It undermines the foundation of my security and it also touches on my well-known issue around acceptance. I depend on others for my security when it needs to come from within.

As a result I decided not to take things personally and to allow others to express their opinion in my presence or absence, in other words to practise acceptance some more. In addition I reminded myself to view the opinions of others about others as solely their perception or interpretation held in that particular instance. I also vowed to strive not to form an opinion about others. Most crucially and significantly I determined to access my Core Self as the basis of my support, acceptance and sense of security and esteem. Pursuit of this was immensely freeing and has served me extremely well.

Example 9

At one stage I noticed that I reacted sensitively to the accusation 'This is all your fault'. Intellectually I did not feel guilty or ashamed, because I did not accept the concepts of 'fault' or 'wrong', nor did I agree with the others' assessment. Yet I was irritated and annoyed on each occasion at being told that I was responsible. Therefore I decided that some investigation was called for. I asked myself: 'Why am I offended by this, when intellectually it seems irrelevant? Why do I make it into an issue?'

Staying with those questions for a while, in a quiet moment, I sensed great unease, apprehension and even fear. The next question was: 'What am I frightened of?' In a flash I became aware of the underlying, immensely retarding, yet powerful notion that, if I was at fault or failed, then I forfeited my right to exist. 'To be or not to be' was at the root of those intense emotions. I was totally astounded and taken aback that I harboured such a grotesque idea within me. I resolved to reinforce with utmost intensity the belief that 'to be' was a given, a divine right, irrespective of what I did or did not do. I was worthwhile, whatever my achievements.

Example 10
Another of my main sources of immense pain was the perceived sense of not being able to connect with others on a deep enough level. I used to become quite upset when I met with close relatives and the interactions stayed on a superficial level. All my attempts to connect on a more intimate level generally failed. This also happened to some degree in my partner relationships and friendships.

Initially I was just very dissatisfied and disappointed with the interactions. Later the lack of sufficient connection became quite upsetting. I asked myself:

Why do I feel so dissatisfied, frustrated and hurt about my interactions with X, Y or Z?
    Realization: There is a deep yearning within me to connect more deeply with those people.
    Question: What is this showing me?

As I stayed with this question I realised that what was missing was a more intimate relationship with my Inner Part, Centre or Core Self. The pain around my shallow relationship with others was alerting me to a deep, unconscious yearning for a more consciously aware, profound relationship with my Essence or

Spirit Aspect. It became clear to me that I needed to make this a high priority. As I started to reach out and get in touch with my Core Self (more about this in Part 3), my frustration around the lack of depth in my relationships with others lessened and then disappeared, although I still appreciate and enjoy a deep connection when I encounter one.

Example 11

I noticed that I became angry when it was insinuated that others are so much more equipped or in a better position than I to know what is the most appropriate concept, attitude or behaviour. I rebelled strongly against the notion that I should follow the common practice and toe the line. On some reflection regarding this issue I decided to trust my inner knowing, because the following points made sense to me:

o The common practice often varies from culture to culture and is therefore not always as 'common' as it is intimated.

o History has proven that the majority is not always 'in-the-know' of the 'truth' per se or is necessarily pursuing the most beneficial action.

o There would be no progress without the emergence of original or 'uncommon' ideas or concepts.

o On what authority should somebody know better than I do what is right for me?

My sensitivity in this area showed me my own doubts and confusion with respect to this aspect and my need to explore where I stood and to make a conscious, fully aware decision.

The exploration of my annoyance around constantly being told what to do raised the question for me: When is it appropriate to persist in doing what feels right for us, and when do we compromise or modify our actions and communications to accommodate others? My conclusions are:

It depends on how important and essential the activity is for us and for the other. Honest, frank negotiations, sponsored by good-will, will help. Another crucial factor, as with most decisions, is: Does the wish for the action or interaction come from our Ego or from our Core Self? To discern whether it is an Ego aspect or our Core Self which is sponsoring our choice, we only need to survey our body sensations and check whether we are experiencing feelings of ease and comfort or feelings of discomfort and unease.

As a consequence of my conclusions I resolved to be more tolerant and accepting of other people's opinions and choices and to fully own my choices.

Example 12
The following example illustrates that sometimes an enquiry can yield instantaneous and profound changes.

Not so long ago an incident evoked hurt and sadness around the perception of not being paid attention to and taken care of. I longed for somebody close to me to be fully present and aware of me. When I looked into what this situation was showing me, I realised that I am looking in the 'wrong' place for attention. I am requiring presence and awareness of people who are unable to be there for me, because they are too wrapped up in themselves and too preoccupied with their own issues.

> *Question:* Why am I seeking attention from people who are in that moment unable to be available?
> *Answer:* To highlight and bring out into the open my imaginary conviction that I am not being paid attention to and taken care of.

> *Question:* What is the message in this for me?

Like a flash of lightning I became profoundly and experientially aware that I am already grandly taken care of. All my needs are met. I am not lacking anything. All that I require I already have. This was a sudden, huge and extremely powerful revelation for me. It produced a tremendous shift. Although I had known this to some extent intellectually, I felt it now at a deep level; it had become a certainty. All that was left to do was to keep this understanding alive and ever-present in my everyday awareness. Realisations can sometimes easily slip into the background.

Although this was just another incident to highlight the issue of not being paid attention to and being cared for, it brought me a different realisation rather than the usual reminder to pay more attention to my Essence. Many different incidents may lead us to the same core issue. Yet sometimes processing the emotions around a well-established core issue may lead to a new revelation. This example also exemplifies how the exploration of our emotions may procure an instantaneous shift in our clarity. Sometimes a change occurs by itself, without any effort on our part.

You may say that we can always make up an answer. My response is this:

o This insight provided the impetus for an enormously helpful and worthwhile shift.
o Even if we make it all up, if it moves us past an issue, if it improves our life and brings us more freedom, peace, more of what we want, then it is useful in its own right.

Processing our feelings in this way does facilitate all that and it ensures that we address that which at that time is most important and beneficial for us to deal with.

These are a few of the ways I dealt with my emotions over a period of many years. The method slowly evolved into the process described in the previous chapter.

Although the application of the process will vary from person to person, there are a few distinctive and crucial features, which form a central part of the process:

o We understand and appreciate that our negative emotions alert us that something is amiss in our viewpoints or way of being. An uncomfortable emotion indicates that we are harbouring an idea which is not in our best interests and which is out of step with who we are in Essence.
o We heed the signal and ferret out the counterproductive perspective or attitude.
o We modify the detrimental sentiment or way of being; we change our mind.

o We reinforce our new perspective, especially when our emotions alert us that the old perspective has surfaced again.

Our feelings and what catches our attention will bring us back again and again to the same issue until that particular issue is completely transformed. Each time we process our emotions we will gain further understanding and wisdom or experience a shift in our needs and definitely become more liberated and empowered. One by one each issue becomes transformed, bringing as a result immense freedom, peace, contentment and tremendous joy and elation.

1.8 Examples of the key understanding I have gained as a result of processing my emotions

Although a major part of this book has emerged from my understanding and insights gained from processing my negative emotions, I want to summarise some of the immediate and most crucial understanding and insights I have gathered from my processes.

What I have learned from:

o My issues around **acceptance:**
   Processing the pain that I have experienced, because I felt not accepted, I have come to realise that I was withholding to a stark degree from myself and others, that which I was unsuccessfully seeking from significant others. I so wanted those around me to accept me as I was and **yet** I did not accept myself to a large degree. I expected others to give me that which I was not prepared to give myself. Equally, I did not give others what I wished from them. This was a huge eye-opener for me.

   Secondly, I have become deeply aware how much my need for acceptance is limiting me. It made me dependent on others for my emotional or psychological well-being. I also realised that my requirement for approval was an unfair imposition on others. In addition, as I became more accepting of myself, I became less needy of others' recognition and I noticed that I was a great deal more widely accepted than it previously appeared.

   Thirdly, I have come to appreciate what a precious gift my extension of acceptance is to the other. I have come to grasp at a deep, experiential level that to accept another just as he/she is (the good, the bad and the ugly), without any preconditions, is the essence of love. It is what love is all about.

This is in stark contrast to the love I have seen displayed. The love I have observed and experienced so far was more given out of a need of the giver rather than for the benefit of the receiver. I have also seen it frequently used as a tool for manipulation and control. It was liberally bestowed, when one did the 'right' action and swiftly and unremittingly withheld, when one did the 'wrong' action. As a result of this understanding I resolved, with great intention, to be at peace with myself and others just as we are right now. To do so was not easy because my deeply ingrained modus operandi was to constantly berate my actions and efforts. Equally I had to repeatedly remind myself to allow others to be and do what they want to when I considered their actions unwise or self-defeating. Yet should they be open to my suggestions, I would offer my understanding.

In conclusion the processing of my huge hurt and pain, generated from my issues around the theme of acceptance, afforded me with an immense learning and clarity around what it means to accept myself or another, and its impor-tance, and it motivated me hugely to do my utmost to accept myself and others more completely.

o My issue around being **misjudged** and **not** being **recognised**: I frequently experienced considerable anger and grief when I perceived myself as being misjudged and not seen. Processing those feelings I realised how important it was for me to address the issue of assessing myself and others negatively and of being blind to what there is to see. As a result I vowed to pay particular attention to any signs of me judging myself and others and to endeavour to see and acknowledge all of myself, especially my Authentic, Intrinsic Self and to do the same for others.

There is a difference between judgement and observation. Observation is noticing something without attaching a value such as 'good' or 'bad' to it. Judging is adding ourselves, our preferences, to what we notice. We give it a value such as 'right' or 'wrong', 'nice' or 'nasty', 'good' or 'bad'.

Being recognised and validated very powerfully promotes a feel-good experience. It certainly is very seductive. Irrespective of this, however, I resolved to let go of my need to be recognised by others. Much later I realised that once I had learned to validate myself and my intrinsic nature, my need for this automatically receded and eventually vanished.

o My confusion and misunderstanding around **responsibility**: Issues relating to responsibility had surfaced many times as the core subject of painful incidents. I soon realised that this was a crucial issue for me. After a great deal of reflection I eventually fully embraced the understanding that:

a) I am fully responsible for what is in my life, every last bit of it.

b) Others are not responsible for me. Without realising it I considered others as inconsiderate or uncaring when they did not comply with my requirements and needs.

c) In return, others are responsible for what is in their life and I must respect that and accept their choices. I always felt compelled to make it 'alright' for others. Yet my 'assistance and help' often met with resistance or it drained and frustrated me. Furthermore, my interventions to alleviate pain often compromised following my own inner promptings. Eventually I had to acknowledge that my assistance was not always in the best interests of the other, but rather came from an Ego-need of mine.

Yet there may be occasions, when our assistance is of benefit to others. In such a case it is advisable to do our utmost to help. Whether our action is prompted by an unhelpful Ego-sponsored urge to intervene, because we consider the other person's choice as not being in their best interests, or whether our deed is in line with our Core Self and thus beneficial, we can ascertain by observing our body sensations or feelings. Feelings of ease and joy mean that the proposed action is beneficial to the other. Feelings of apprehension, unease, heaviness, reluctance or dread means that the action is not in the overall best interests of the other, but is motivated by a particular Ego aspect.

o The understanding I gained with respect to the **victim stance**: I have experienced immense frustration and grief as a result of those close to me playing the victim in numerous ways. My resentment was a product of the fact that the victim scenario displayed by others powerfully meshed with my need to take care of others and to see others happy. Processing the discomfort which seemed to originate from others adopting the victim role, made me aware that I myself played the victim to a considerable extent. In addition, I became aware how patronising it was of me to view others as in 'need' of 'rescue'. As a consequence of this insight I vowed to see the 'victims' in my life (including myself) as powerful, able and independent.

Working with and reflecting on my role as a victim and observing what was around me helped me to deeply grasp key aspects of the victim mentality. It also made me sensitive and alert to signs of me slipping back into the victim role. Here are some of the crucial features of the victim role, which I have identified as a result of the above: common to all aspects of victimhood is the element of choice. As victims we are partially or completely unaware of some of the perspectives, judgements or attitudes we have chosen in the past and which have a bearing on the unwelcome situation or occurrence we encounter now. In addition we are partially or totally oblivious of the huge range of perspectives available to us with regard to the presently experienced negative event.

In this context there are three distinct aspects to our choices:
1. We are continuously met with the consequences of our past choices by way of the reactions of others or events or circumstances.

2. When we meet up with and experience the reactions, events, circumstances, which we set in motion through our past choices, we in response adopt (consciously or unconsciously) a particular perspective or opinion. In turn how we choose to view the unsettling event determines how we feel.

3. In turn the perspective, thought and attitude we have opted for determine the happenings we line up for the future.

We are constantly faced with endless choices. The crucial factor is a) how aware we are of the various points of view available to us and b) how aware we are of the particular perspective or notion we have made our own. A significant characteristic of the victim stance is that we have partial or no awareness of point a and/or b. The consequence of this often is that we take little or no responsibility for what we encounter.

Because as victims we are oblivious of our past choices and their bearing on the present situation, we perceive the unpleasant incidents we meet with as unlucky, random or unfair. In addition, because we are unaware of the wide range of options available in relation to the situation we find ourselves in, we believe the conditions or circumstances are outside of our control. Since we see ourselves unable to influence the unpleasant situation we feel powerless. To compensate for this lack of internal power we may resort to external power. Thus as victims we often engage in blaming, emotional manipulation or other means of coercion. In addition, our conviction of being wronged or unfairly treated serves to justify all manner of uncaring verbal outpourings or actions.

Why we choose the victim role:

o Initially it can be difficult to spot the fact that we are operating in victim mode, because we are so out of touch with our choices. Thus we feel so vindicated in our disappointment, outrage, indignation, disgust, resentment, frustration, hate, in our sense of being misjudged, injured, violated, in our sense of it all being totally uncalled for. We are so caught up in our perception of it all coming from and happening out there, completely oblivious of our input and our response-ability to it.

o For some victims the drama can seem quite captivating and alluring with all the energies in rapid motion. There are many who thrive on this aspect of the drama.

o Being in the victim role may sometimes seem a very good place to be. It allows us to remain passive and to become reinless, unrequired passengers. We are not required to confront our less than helpful perspectives and attitudes and we are exempt from making maybe initially inconvenient changes.

o The victim stance is popular and widespread and we are generally well supported in this role by others. As victims we are showered with much-wanted attention and sympathy. Thus we do not only have to overcome our own hurdles in the form of misguided perceptions, but we also have to swim against the tide of victim culture.

o Playing the victim we are exempt from 'making mistakes' (mistakes in the sense that we have created something we did not intend to create), because as the victim 'we have no choice'. 'Making mistakes' may be judged as failure and thus might lock into an existing deep buried sense of not being good enough or being worthless. Judging 'mistakes' negatively or as an indication of our lack of worth may cause us to abdicate our responsibility for the original choice and we choose to see ourselves as victims instead.

o We may also enter into the victim role because we see ourselves as incompetent or weak and we try to cajole others to compensate for the perceived deficiency.

The downside of the victim role:

Playing the victim may elicit much-wanted sympathy, attention, approval and support from others, which may appear to serve us well temporarily, but we lose heavily in the long run. Victimhood comes at a high price. The price is considerable limitation and immense disempowerment. Whilst in the victim mode we negate our innate power and render ourselves powerless. We abdicate our right and ability to create for ourselves the life we want to live and to be who we want to be. The result is always further pain and misery and far more negative effects than the ones we tried to avoid in the first place.

In addition, as a result of processing a profuse number of negative emotions:

o I realised how little I was available to others, when my own issues were triggered, and how much I missed of what was conveyed to me, because I had 'switched off' and darted into assumptions.

o I have come to appreciate that my childhood experiences led me to and highlighted precisely those thoughts and misguided beliefs which were most detrimental to my psychological well-being and therefore most in need of change and transformation. The same childhood environment affected my brother quite differently.

o I slowly recognised how deep-seated and persistent some of my originally unconsciously held ideas were. For example a small part of me still harbours the idea that I am incompetent. However, when I am in touch with my Authentic Self, my competence is not in question.

o I have come to appreciate to what extent our so-called negative feelings may be used as a brilliant tool to discover our unconscious perspectives and attitudes, our unknown views, beliefs or judgements or to become aware of those orientations, ways of being and operating or those patterns of relating and interacting which we are oblivious to. In short, I more and more realised the immensely helpful, powerful capacity of our uncomfortable emotions to get to know ourselves intimately. I found the processing of my negative emotions an enormously fascinating and captivating journey of discovery, unfolding right in front of me.

1.9 The conclusions I have arrived at as a result of my processes and my reflections on the arising insights

I want to share some of the understanding I have arrived at as a result of deliberately processing my uncomfortable, undesirable emotions and experiences and as a consequence of reflecting more deeply on the aspects which have surfaced as a result of my processing.

❖ I have come to realise that:

o There is only one enemy we have and that is our misunderstanding and confusion.

o The most difficult person to meet with is ourselves and yet the meeting with ourselves is the most rewarding, interesting, exciting, the most powerful and liberating pursuit.

o Our tormentors and chains are our erroneous judgements and assumptions, our unconscious, unexamined beliefs and attitudes.

o Something is whatever I make it. Something does not matter, unless I make it matter. I recommend that we examine why we make something matter.

o If something gets our attention, then there is something there to inform us and to be gained. The question is only how much gain we allow in.

o All 'negative' judgements and 'labelling' originate from misunderstanding and confusion. They always diminish the one who makes the judgement.

o There are two aspects to any unwelcome event or situation:

One aspect is that the other(s) are unhelpful or non-beneficial in their interaction(s) or that the incident or circumstance is inconvenient or at variance with our desires and intentions.

The other facet is that what we make of the inopportune situation or occurrence is up to us. We may view it in a way which causes us to be furious, frustrated or disappointed or we adopt a viewpoint which causes us to be peaceful, at ease or elated. Also the incident affords us an opportunity to address an aspect, a habit, an attitude or a way of being, which is not in our best interests.

o By holding on to a sense of being 'wronged' and our resentment around it, we keep that 'wrong-doing' alive and kicking and decidedly a part of our make-up. In fact, every time our thoughts return to that incident and we reinforce our judgements around it, we add to that 'wound' and enlarge the build-up of energy associated with it. Allowing ourselves to feel the hurt and deciding to change our mind, removes the issue. This act brings in its wake insights, increased freedom and peace of mind.

o When a particular situation persists in our life and it causes negative emotions, it is useful to ask ourselves: 'What is it that escapes me here?' 'What am I not seeing?'

o When I am complaining about an attitude or way of being of another I find, on reflection, that the aspect of the complaint is something I myself need to address or change.

o Sometimes the glaringly obvious is right in front of us and we look right past it. Others can see it, because it is not their issue or impeding notion. It is our negative judgement that leads us to become blind to the blatantly obvious. Sometimes other people will support us in our blindness, for their own ulterior motives, such as to elicit our support for their blind spots.

o When I feel dislike towards another person, I know I am focusing on a particular aspect of the other which is activating or interacting with one of my Ego aspects; maybe something is mirrored which I unconsciously disown. If I were focused on the Core Self of the other, I would not see anything to be disliked. Likewise, if I were in Core Self mode myself, then I could not perceive any lack or fault in the other.

o When somebody communicates with us, then that person

shares with us a part of his or her world. The other is making public a part of his or her understanding, perspective or belief. What somebody says and does is a statement of who he or she chooses to be at that moment and **NOT** a statement of who we are, unless we make it so. It is about him or her and **NOT** about us. However what **we do** with his/her communication is about **us**; it is a **statement of who we choose to be at that moment.**

o We may allow the communication of others to limit us or to liberate us, to bring us pain or insights and understanding. Whether the communication is meant to be supportive or not, we can gain in both cases.

o Others may unintentionally trigger our emotions:
We already harbour a detrimental notion or viewpoint and therefore the potential for our emotions to be set in motion is in place.
The other has done us a favour by bringing this issue to our attention and thus has given us an opportunity to amend an unhelpful idea.

o Alternatively, others may intentionally 'press our buttons':
The other is under the spell of an unhelpful perspective and not aware of the whole picture; he/she perceives him/herself as the injured party and thus justifies his/her attack.
Whether another brings up an issue intentionally or unintentionally is of little importance. What is important is that we ourselves use the opportunity to discover and rectify a detrimental notion, perspective or attitude.

❖ When an 'unwelcome' incident happens we may:
either lament it, blame ourselves, somebody or something for it, resist it, become angry, outraged, frustrated, resentful, disappointed, adopt the victim role and plump into self-pity or regret *or*
we may choose to see it from a different perspective and decide that this is an opportunity to move on, to evolve, to let go of something outdated or unhelpful, to acquire a new understanding or a new way of being. It might be useful to

affirm: 'I will gain from this'; 'I will find meaning'; 'I will find a way to make it enrich my life.'

❖ While it is comforting and supporting when somebody notices us, listens attentively, sees us fully, is patient, caring, considerate and we need to thoroughly appreciate and enjoy it when it happens, it is extremely empowering and liberating to get to a place where we are at ease without those qualities being extended to us. Yet when we bestow those attributes towards others we will automatically become independent of the need to be, for example, noticed or validated.

❖ When we deliberately process our emotions as described previously we gain an experiential, deep-level understanding of what is involved in being, for example, unconditionally accepting, compassionate, or available. We get under the skin of those ways of being or qualities and internalise the nature of what, for example, acceptance entails, especially when we encounter the same issue repeatedly. We grasp its essence beyond its mere intellectualisation and we come to recognise it when we see it.

❖ I found particularly revealing and astounding my realisation that the comments and behaviour of others, which I found so hurtful, were something I did myself, but was totally blind to. I reacted negatively to precisely the way of being that I was exhibiting myself, but unconsciously disowned. Although I did not like the idea that I was doing that which on a conscious level I abhorred, I found this revelation nonetheless extremely illuminating and powerful.

❖ I realised that it is usually easy to spot the apparently erroneous or counterproductive beliefs, attitude or behaviour taken on by others. They seem obvious to us and we may be amazed that the other cannot see the contradiction between their actions and their desires or the self-creation of their demise. It is much more difficult to become fully aware of our

own counterproductive ideas and beliefs. For one, we assume
that how we see something is the only sensible, 'real' way of
perceiving it. Another and particularly deceptive aspect is the
fact that our experiences seem to validate our ideas or judgements. They serve as confirmation of and justification for
maintaining our limiting or detrimental beliefs. This creates a
vicious cycle. However, the cycle starts with the choosing of our
opinions or notions and not with our experience of the event,
because we first decide on the meaning and then we live
through the incident in a certain way. Future experiences of
similar occurrences or situations will fall in line with our
previous interpretation of them.

Yet we may exit this cycle of endless repetition of negative
experiences by paying close attention to our feelings and exploring the accompanying thoughts giving rise to the feelings.
Instead of seeing the experience as proof of our belief, we
examine the usefulness or validity of our adopted viewpoint.
Our perspectives are not a reflection of 'reality' or 'truth' per se.
Our 'truth' is formed by the assessment or meaning we choose
and our future experiences will confirm our truth for us, because
we view the new experience through the lens of our past judgements, filtering out all other viewpoints or perspectives.

❖ Notwithstanding that suffering is self-created, we still need
to empathise with our own and the distress of another. We all
can relate to pain. Pain can be an extremely unpleasant or debilitating experience, however much it is self-inflicted, and it
deserves our compassion. We need to hold out whatever will
comfort and support the other.

Yet there are two points to keep hold of:
Firstly there is a difference between empathy and sympathy.
This difference may be illustrated symbolically. When someone
is in a deep pit, we can either jump in the hole with him/her,
which symbolises the action of sympathy, or we can hand the
person in the hole a rope or a ladder, which symbolises
the action of empathy. When we empathise we keep hold of the

larger picture and do not adopt the perspective of the person in the pit and thus our assistance is much more effective.

Secondly, whilst assisting and supporting the other we must not loose sight of the notion that the other always has a choice. We must refrain from seeing the other as powerless and thus potentially undermine his/her power.

❖ Our emotions are a brilliant guidance system. When we experience so-called positive emotions, we know we are on track and co-operating with our Essence. When we are experiencing so-called negative emotions, we know we are out of step with our Core Self. We have opted for something which is not in our best interests and which is off-course with who we are in Essence. This may be a notion, judgement, perspective or attitude, which we have adopted now or in the past. Often we are not aware of the ideas we have taken on board or conclusions we have come to and they then form part of our unconscious. Thus our feelings can be used to discover our unconscious aspects.

❖ It may take great courage to acknowledge and own something we dislike or judge negatively. It is often easier to resort to blaming, being self-righteous, feeling outraged or resentful or turning a blind eye. Does doing so serve us well? No, not in the long run. It keeps our unhelpful notions and patterns in place replaying the same issues endlessly, albeit maybe in different contexts and disguises. It deadens us. It robs us of enthusiasm and aliveness. It deprives us of experiencing a far richer, more interesting, expansive, rewarding life. Getting to know ourselves is an amazing, infinitely interesting, fascinating journey of discovery, full of unexpected vistas. At the final destination we arrive at our Essence and we can immerse ourselves in its full beauty, peace and freedom.

❖ I greatly appreciate what my pain has afforded me. Working with my painful emotions has turned my life around and brought me to a good place to be. Yet, we do not have to go through the route of pain to gain understanding or to grow and evolve. We may also achieve this without pain by a) paying keen attention to what is in front of us and allowing it to inform us about ourselves and the nature of the universe and b) becoming still and listening to the whispers of the wisdom inside us.

1.10 In Essence

Anything can inform us about ourselves and the content of our unconscious. However, our emotions are an immensely clear, immediate, reliable, unfailing medium to highlight what is not working. In this respect they are one of the fastest and most powerful methods to surpass what is hindering us in achieving our deep-seated desires and to move rapidly into increasing freedom, fulfilment, joy and peace.

Our negative emotions are due to a limited or incomplete understanding. At the same time they are an opening to a better understanding and they provide easy access to our unconscious.

Our uncomfortable emotions always have **to do with us** and **not** to do with anybody else or any situation or circumstance. The only element which generates any uncomfortable emotion, is an unhelpful perspective or way of being that we are entertaining. Circumstances are neutral until we decide what they mean. Yet in the moment of deciding on a meaning we dress up the circumstance and give it a specific flavour. Thus our emotions denote the flavour we have chosen; they indicate the degree of helpfulness of our viewpoint or thought.

We can demote or promote our feelings at any stage by changing our mind. We may deliberately modify or redirect our thoughts, outlook or way of being in a manner which causes the elevation of our feelings. We may incrementally elevate or promote our emotions by searching for and adopting increasingly better-feeling notions until we reach the level of immense exhilaration, profound peace and unbounded freedom.

When we process our negative emotions we generate more desirable and elevated feelings and experiences and we reduce the volume of our unhelpful thoughts and beliefs. When we do not process our uncomfortable feelings we line up more unpleasant experiences for some future occasion and we expand our detrimental perspectives.

Our emotions represent a direct line of communication from our Core Self. They indicate to what degree our choice of meaning or attitude is divorced from who we are in Essence; they reveal to what extent we are siding in our interactions and thoughts with our Core Self or a misguided Ego part. In this capacity our emotions may serve as a powerful, effective tool for decreasing our unhelpful Ego aspects and increasing our Core way of Being.

So what do I mean by Ego and Core Self and what are the distinguishing features of each? Whereas Part 1 focused on our emotions, their significance and value, Part 2 focuses on the characteristics and the relevance of our Core Self and our Ego aspects.

Part 2

Ego versus
Core Self

2.1 What do I mean by Ego and Core Self?

I define the **Ego** here as the accumulation of those of our thoughts, perspectives, interpretations, attitudes and ways of being which are at variance with our most cherished intentions and desires and which are incompatible with who we are in Essence. Our Ego parts as defined here are generated by and a representation of the meanings we have given occurrences, the conclusions we have arrived at, the ideas and notions we have taken on board, the values, criteria and ways of being we have adopted which are less than helpful and to a varying degree detrimental to our overall well-being.

We may not be aware of some or many of our Ego parts because, unless we are in the habit of reflectively observing our thoughts and communications or processing our uncomfortable emotions, many of our choices will have been made unconsciously, without clear awareness.

I define the **Core Self** or Essence as who we are at the Core of our Being, our authentic, intrinsic, essential, unconditioned, unimpeded Self. Our Core Self is absolute consciousness and awareness, perfect balance, immeasurable potential, total ease, peace and stillness, all-encompassing wisdom, complete clarity and understanding, monumental freedom and power, infinite appreciation, pure joy, inexhaustible enthusiasm and passion and eternal bliss to name but a few characteristics. Sometimes it is referred to as Soul or Spirit. The Core Self is common to all of us and contains the same characteristics for all of us.

When we are in the **Ego** state:

o We experience 'negative' feelings such as doubt, shame,

regret, distrust; we are angry, depressed, jealous, over-whelmed, disappointed, worried or fearful amongst others.

o We entertain perspectives, notions or ways of being which are incompatible with our Core Self.
o We act unconsciously.
o We limit ourselves in what we think is possible or what we believe we can do or achieve. We are less than what we can be.
o Our communications and actions are not benefiting others.
o We create for our future more negative, uncomfortable experiences.
o Our sense of worth and our confidence are impaired.
o Our sense of aliveness, our energy, passion or enthusiasm are diminished.
o We operate in a reactive mode; we impulsively, without reflection or deliberation, react in response to outside or even inside stimuli rather than proactively making a conscious, deliberate choice.

When we are in the **Core Self** state:

o We experience 'positive' feelings; we are eager, at ease, peaceful, optimistic, enthusiastic, passionate, appreciative, powerful or joyful amongst others.
o We engage in perspectives, thoughts or ways of being which are compatible or congruent with our Essence.
o We act consciously, with awareness.
o We place no limitations on what we consider possible.
o Our communications and actions are beneficial to others.
o We create desirable experiences for ourselves.
o We appreciate and acknowledge without reservation our worth and our confidence is not restricted in any way.
o We feel full of life, well-being, energy, zest and passion.
o We operate in a creative mode; we consciously and deliber-ately decide what an occurrence or interaction means and our response to it.

So, in our daily life, how do the perspective, attitude or way of being of our Ego aspects differ from those of our Core Self?

2.2 Comparing our Ego aspects with the Core Self way of being

The variety of Ego aspects is limitless because the choice of limiting notions is limitless. The amount of Ego parts each individual may make their own varies hugely from no Ego aspects (generally very rare) to an immense conglomerate of Ego parts. In order to highlight the differences in perspective and way of being between a large collection of Ego parts and that of a unified Core Self (referred to below as 'Core') I contrast below the responses or ways of being with regards to various aspects of our life:

Awareness, understanding and clarity versus confusion and misconceptions.

Ego   The Ego would not exist in the presence of full awareness. Our misguided assumptions and judgements, our skewed beliefs, our imaginings and illusions are generated in the field of partial awareness and understanding. Because the Ego is full of doubt, confusion and uncertainty it looks outside of itself for direction and clarity.

Assumptions and beliefs are adopted without exploring their validity. Once we have made a belief our own, then our experiences will seemingly verify our beliefs. For example when we feel we are not loved we interpret the behaviour, action and utterance of others in line with that belief. Thus our assumption that we are not loved is apparently confirmed by our experience. It can be quite difficult to break out of this vicious cycle and to pierce through this spell of our own making, because it seems so obvious, undisputable and real to us. The way past our illusions is conscious awareness and the tools discussed in Part 1.

Core   The Core Self operates with clear and complete conscious awareness, without any mental distortions or modifications. It perceives clearly and acutely what is so without fashioning any value judgements.

When we are aligned with our Core Self we operate from the base of our own innate knowing. We reach within ourselves for answers, understanding and clarity. We invest time exploring and gaining insights. We do not adopt others' beliefs and ideas without checking them out with our own truth. Yet we remain open to immediately modifying or changing our truth in the face of any new understanding or insights accessed from yet more elevated levels within ourselves.

Internal power and mastery versus external power and control

Ego   When we are in the Ego state we are unaware of or disconnected from our own **internal** power. To compensate for this perceived powerlessness and the resulting fears and insecurities we **grasp** for **external** power and exert control. This manifests in resorting to manipulation, coercion, emotional blackmail, intimidation, deception, divisiveness, scheming, pretence, seducing, subterfuge and competitiveness amongst others.

Core   The Core Self is the **essence** of **internal** power. Therefore the Core Self has **no need** for **external** power and defensiveness. When we function in unison with our Core Self, we acknowledge and respect the boundaries and choices of others. We are also fully open and transparent, because we feel safe and have nothing to guard against.

Freedom versus limitations

Ego   The Ego is **limited** in many ways. One impeding element is the Ego's inhibiting beliefs and notions. Another limiting aspect is that whilst we are in the Ego state, we are disconnected from our source of complete understanding, clarity, power and freedom and thus we are constrained by many perceived needs and insecurities. We tend to look to others to meet our needs and thus are dependent on others. Likewise, whilst in Ego mode we are in many respects outer or other-determined. We are looking for our choices to be validated and approved by others.

Many of our Ego aspects do not respect the freedom of others.

Core   The Core Self is totally **free** from any limitations and hindrances. It has no needs and is thus independent of others.

It holds out total freedom to others, fully respecting their choices.

Love versus fear

Ego   Fear arises out of a limited or incomplete understanding. Most Ego-sponsored thoughts, communications and actions are fear-based. Fear comes in the form of perceived vulnerability, insufficiency, isolation or disconnectedness. Thus when operating in the Ego state we are on guard and defensive; we contract and limit our experiences.

Love in its truest sense is acceptance. The Ego perceives imperfections in itself and others and rejects parts of itself and others. Thus in its non-acceptance it does not practise love in the purest form. Feelings of love are sponsored by a person's own needs, sense of incompleteness or by feeling insecure or bored. Love becomes a trade-off. It is **conditional**, because it is given with requirements or conditions attached. When acting from an Ego aspect, our love is often impeding the other; it is manipulative or restrictive.

Core   When we are fully connected with our Core Self we are in touch with our deep inner knowing where there is no room for fear and all its manifestations.

The thoughts, communications, actions, and way of being of the Core Self are love-based. The love is born out of the knowledge and understanding of our true nature, which is freedom, peace, appreciation and acceptance. The Core Self is fully accepting of Self and others and it has no needs. Thus, from the place of our Core Self we can give love without requiring anything back or without making conditions; we give love **unconditionally**. Love from the Core Self perspective is supportive, beneficial, enhancing, up-lifting, freeing.

Trust and intimacy versus suspicion and disconnectedness.

Ego   Due to its patchy understanding the Ego entity lacks trust towards itself, others, life and the universe. Events appear to happen randomly, without discernable pattern or rationale.

Therefore the universe appears to be full of uncertainty and quite unpredictable. As a result of a sense of exposure to uncontrollable and potentially malignant forces and thus a sense of vulnerability and fear, our connection to and intimacy with others is impaired.

Core   The Core Self has a sound sense of trust, trusting that life or the universe are supportive and beneficial. It is certain that there is a benign organising power behind everything.

When operating in a Core Self state we feel safe and therefore there is no need to guard against others. Thus we are able to connect with others and the universe to a high degree and on a deep level; we are open and accessible.

Ownership and responsibility versus disowning one's choices

Ego   The Ego takes no or only partial responsibility for its own choices and the resulting negative experiences. For the Ego entity the cause for the effects it experiences lies outside of itself. It does not realise that the occurrences or situations it encounters were influenced or generated by its thoughts, attitudes and deeds. Thus the Ego places the ownership or 'fault' for the unwelcome incidents and the accompanying emotions on the shoulders of others, fate or life and it resorts to blaming, retaliating or feeling victimised.

Core The Core Self takes full responsibility for everything in its life, for its choices and their consequences, for its experiences, actions, communications and thoughts. When we operate on course with our Core Self, we are aware of and accept that we are the cause of all that we encounter.

Reactor versus creator

Ego   When we are in the Ego state, we operate as a **reactor**. A reactor responds to outside stimuli such as the actions or utterances of others or to the emotions he/she experiences, without conscious deliberation and aware choices. Instead he/she acts out his/her own emotions.
Often the actions governed by our Ego do not take us where we wish to be or further that which we wish to achieve.

Core When in the Core Self state, we operate as a **creator**. A creator responds consciously, with full awareness. As a creator we give events, circumstances, occurrences consciously and deliberately their meaning and thus create our experiences with intent and full awareness. Our actions and utterances are governed by our carefully chosen priorities and in line with our intentions;

they are motivated by internal factors rather than external factors.

Self-determined versus other-determined

Ego   Because of our uncertainty and doubts, when in the Ego state we look outside for answers and solutions to problems. We seek explanations and solutions from authority figures or experts. In addition, we often have to have our choices validated and approved of by others.

Core   When we are aligned with our Core Self, we acknowledge that we are the supreme authority with respect to our own life and that we have all the answers within ourselves. Therefore we endeavour to access solutions to problems and answers to questions through reaching deep within in quiet, relaxed moments. The validity of any advice offered by others is first examined against our sense of rightness or positive feelings and only then endorsed. We do not need the approval of others (our own self-worth is sufficient) and we are thus independent of others.

Purpose, goals and priorities

Ego   When functioning in line with our Ego entity our goals are often vague and contradictory and do not promote the most fulfilling quality of life.

       We lack well-defined priorities. We generally do not use our time and energy with consistent intention; we use time and energy to a large extent haphazardly and often with a less than helpful effect. We engage in whatever appears most urgent or most dramatic.

Core   For the Core Self life has purpose and meaning. When we are aligned with our Core Self, our aspirations are growth-promoting, inspiring, expansive and enhance our quality of life.

       We set clear, well-defined, deliberate priorities,

chosen for their maximum benefit to self and others and we implement these priorities without distractions and with zeal and enthusiasm. Our energy and time are used with maximum effectiveness towards achieving the chosen goals.

Attention

Ego   The attention of the Ego-governed person is directed by its five senses and captured by the most prominent, dramatic outside stimuli at any moment. Its attention is scattered or random.

Core The attention of the person operating from the Core Self is focused like a laser-beam and directed at will. When we are on course with our Core Self, we penetrate deep into whatever we focus on and we fully concentrate on the object of our attention.

Motivation and commitment

Ego   The Ego entity easily wavers in its motivation, commitment and persistence towards a particular goal, because it is made up of many contradictory agendas. It is also easily waylaid and confused by opposing opinions from others.

Core The Core Self is highly motivated towards and committed to the chosen goals and priorities, since they have originated from the clarity of a unified field and a deep desire within. The Core Self-governed person pursues his/her aspirations with dedication and is not deflected by outside influences.

Reliability and consistency

Ego   Our Ego aspects are made up of many parts with different and often opposing motives and objectives. At various times different Ego parts have the upper hand.

As a result, when we are Ego-governed, we are often unreliable, inconsistent and unpredictable in our responses and actions, because our communications and activities vary according to which Ego part is in the driver's seat.

Core   The Core Self does not consist of conflicting parts; it functions as a homogenous unit. Thus, when we are on course with our Core Self, we are reliable and our responses and actions are consistent.

Integrity and transparency versus disloyalty and secrecy

Ego   The Ego is governed by the need to be accepted, liked, approved of and a sense of being open to harm and thus tends to lack integrity and transparency.

Core   The Core Self does not depend on acceptance or being liked, nor does it lack anything or feel unsafe. Thus when in the Core state, we operate with full integrity and transparency.

Contribution and benefit, giving and receiving

Ego   Generally, when one of our Ego aspects is in the driver's seat, our choices, words and actions do not benefit others directly. They may benefit others indirectly, because we can always use the Ego-sponsored challenges to our advantage. In addition, our issues lessen our availability to others and reduce any contribution we might be able to make. Our Ego-sponsored responses are not specifically selected for their potential benefit to others.

The Ego gives with a hidden agenda or with the purpose of receiving something specifically in return. It also is swallowing up the energy and time and resources of others without giving much of real benefit in return. Instead of contributing, the Ego is lessening or contaminating.

Core   When we function in unison with our Core Self, we
        evaluate and choose any activity and output carefully,
        according to its maximum benefit to self and others; we
        always decide and act with the highest good of self and
        others and the universe in mind.

        Because we are not occupied with issues, we are fully
        available to others. We are giving without an ulterior
        motive or expecting something in return. The giving is
        always to the highest good of others. Moreover, we
        receive with gratitude and grace. Giving and receiving
        are in balance.

Detachment and embracing change versus attachment and resistance

Ego   When in the Ego state we are attached to particular
        outcomes or the presence of particular people, objects or
        environments and we are dependent on having our
        requirements met. Furthermore, we are often not open
        to change; we are reluctant to change our habits, beliefs,
        attitudes or patterns.

Core   When in the Core state we let go easily. We are not
        attached to any particular outcomes or actions of others.
        We are at ease with whatever turns up. In addition, we
        welcome and embrace change with enthusiasm. We
        consider change as part of our evolution.

Perspectives and observations

Ego   Our Ego aspects are generated when we choose perspec-
        tives which are counterproductive to who we want to be
        and what we want to achieve. Those viewpoints are
        frequently adopted unconsciously, without deliberation
        or reflection. Moreover, when in our Ego state our
        observations are coloured or shaped by our adopted
        belief system and judgements.

Core   When we function as one with our Core Self, we adopt our perspectives deliberately and choose only those which are in line with our intentions and aspirations. Our perspectives are geared to promote peace, fulfilment and freedom. Our observation skills are utilised without being clouded by assumptions or past conditionings and they are employed copiously and with keen discernment.

Thoughts and enquiries

Ego   The Ego is made up of thoughts, notions or beliefs. Yet the thoughts constructing the Ego are generally unconscious and always non-beneficial, according to the way I use the term Ego in this book. The thought processes governed by our Ego aspects are usually random, unchecked and unmanaged, copious, often circular or revolving around specific subjects or incidents and generally concerned with the past or the future.

       When in the grip of the Ego the constant chatter and distractions of our thoughts reduce greatly what we are able to observe, our availability to others, and the access to our innate wisdom and knowing. We do not generally engage in deep, meaningful questioning.

Core   Our thoughts, when in a Core Self state, are channelled and focused in line with our conscious priorities. They are deliberate and always peace- and freedom-promoting. They are easily controlled and silenced at will. This allows us to observe acutely and comprehensively, to be fully present and available to others and to have access to our own innate knowing, clarity and wisdom. We ask meaningful questions, seek fundamental answers, we are keen to find out and prepared to see and confront anything that presents itself.

Communications

Ego   Our communications, when in the Ego state, are generally superficial, guarded and often contradictory or ambiguous. In our communications we hide more than we disclose. Also our communications are often conducted with little sensitivity or awareness of the other or of our own assumptions or with little realisation of any higher perspective.

Core   Our communications, when in the Core Self state, reach deep into the core of the subject, are open, revealing, clear, genuine, deliberate and meaningful. They are conducted with considerable awareness of the issues of the other and the consequences and implications of the content of the communication. We connect profoundly with the Core Self of the other.

Inclusiveness and equality versus exclusiveness and inequality

Ego   The Ego consists of a multitude of different parts, each part being seen as distinct and disconnected from all the other parts. Likewise, from the Ego's viewpoint the world and everything in it consists of separate, disconnected units. When in the Ego state we see ourselves to a varying degree as separate from everybody else. This often gives rise to a feeling of isolation and loneliness. The sense of separateness leads to comparison and competition with others. When in the Ego state we usually feel either superior or inferior to others, depending on which Ego part is acting out. We are compelled to belittle others and inflate ourselves to compensate for the lack of self-worth.

Core   The Core Self consists of a single, undivided unit. Likewise, when in a Core Self state, we see ourselves, all others and the world as a unit. Therefore, we feel connected with everything, especially with our Essence; there is no cause for a feeling of loneliness or isolation. Since we do not see ourselves as apart from others, we do not judge ourselves as superior of inferior; we appreciate our worth and view ourselves and others as equally worthwhile.

The above comparisons of the Ego with the Core Self way of being are presented to aid more profound clarity and as a useful tool to discern whether we are siding with one of our Ego aspects or our Core Self. Yet we may always use our feelings as a fast and reliable indicator of which aspect of ours is active or in the driver's seat.

Having contrasted the way of being of a large body of Ego parts with the Core Self way of being, let's focus on the function of the Ego within our overall being and on various aspects of our interactions with it.

2.3 The Ego in various contexts

a) The Ego essentially consists of thoughts and is thus part of our Mind. The Mind is also the organ we use to analyse, investigate, explore, reflect and debate and where our insights, realisations and understanding are registered. Our Ego perspectives and assumptions act like a filter, partly obscuring or screening out and partly modifying or distorting what there is to see.

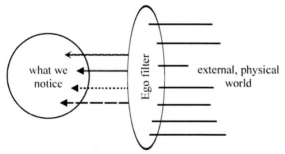

In addition to the Mind, our Being is made up of our Body, which is our physical aspect, and our Core Self or Essence, which is not physical.

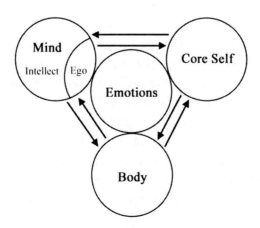

Spatially or physically the various components of our Being are not separate as depicted. However, to illustrate the relationship between those constituents, it is useful to show the units separately.

As depicted in the diagram our Emotions act as a communication link between our three main aspects. Our **Emotions** are signals from our Core Self and they indicate whether a thought, perspective or attitude, adopted in our **Mind,** is beneficial or detrimental to our well-being, whether it is on-course or off-course with our larger truth or who we are at the **Core.** Our **Body** is the place where the Energies in **motion** or **E-motions** are perceived as a whole range of sensations. Our emotions in turn attract specific thoughts.

At times our emotions are messages from our Body to our Mind and Core Self that some aspects of our Body are out of balance or off-course. Bodily dysfunctions are often a reflection of Mind or Thought dysfunctions. Thus illnesses may sometimes serve as a tool to alert us that something needs addressing within our mind or perspectives.

b) We may view our collection of perspectives or Ego aspects as a landscape containing a multitude of distinct features. Likewise, we may liken our emotions to a fluid entity such as an ocean or a river. The above landscape consists of our Core Self district and the various Ego regions. Each Ego aspect of the landscape contains a specific group of ideas, perspectives or attitude.

This landscape or terrain is ever-changing. Whenever we visit a particular part we add to that part or enlarge it; it becomes a more prominent aspect of our being. For this reason it is worthwhile to pay some attention to which part we reside in and thus increase. We may deliberately spend some time in a particular area of our landscape and thus purposefully increase that part.

Whenever we visit an unpleasant part of our landscape, our emotions are somewhere between a choppy, raging ocean and a stagnant, lifeless pool of water. When we reside in the pristine Core Self region of our landscape, our emotions may be likened to a crystal clear, sparkling, playfully gurgling mountain stream or a mirror-like, still lake.

During the course of a day we visit many different zones. We navigate ourselves (consciously or unconsciously) in and out of the diverse regions and in and out of turbulent, choppy waters and calm seas. When we notice at any stage that we are in a particular sector which we do not like or want to be in, we may consciously intervene and deliberately move to another locality, to a locality we prefer. Yet because our Ego areas are often so turbulent and attention captivating, it may at times require considerable effort or strong, deliberate intent to disengage with that boisterous part and redirect our focus to a more calm, harmonious part. The solution here is to strengthen, whenever possible, our quiet but peaceful aspect so that it becomes more prominent and prevalent in our Being and our daily interactions.

c) At any given moment, one or a combination of our parts may be acting out. With regards to a particular incident several of our varied aspects may respond or become active. For example a friend opts out of a planed excursion. One part of us, part X, may take the cancellation personally and feel rejected and not good enough. Another part, part Y, may be glad for the time thus freed up to do a much-wanted long-postponed project. Yet another part, part Z, may be disappointed because it wanted to visit this specific place now. One of the parts may have the upper hand one moment, but the next second another aspect may be in the driver's seat.

I had a friend who was very unpredictable, randomly chopping and changing his attitude, comments, feelings and behaviour with respect to a particular problem. One minute his compassionate aspect had the upper hand and he was very understanding and sympathetic with his daughter, who faced a particular difficulty. Yet some time later he would be driven by fear and allow his anger to gush forth and he became coercive and manipulative. Yet another time, he was disappointed and depressed with respect to the same situation.

We may roughly quantify the amount of overall prominence a particular aspect has with respect to that specific situation. For example, in the situation involving part X, Y, and Z above, part X may have on average 25% prominence of our focus with regard to the incident in question, part Y 60 % prominence, part Z 5% and our Core Aspect 10%. Again we may at any stage purposefully intervene and override the unconscious default percentage. We may place the perspective of our conscious choice at the forefront and give it the leading role.

We need to become a deliberate, conscious director or conductor, who orchestrates all our aspects and parts. We need to determine and decree who gets a high profile and who a low profile, who is called into action and who will take a backseat or who will be transformed altogether. If we do not consciously and deliberately intervene, we chop and change and are aimlessly tossed about like a small boat on a choppy ocean.

d) There are three kinds of interactions possible between the Ego entities and the Core Selves of two people e.g. those of John and Lucy:

1. The Interaction of one Core Self with another Core Self

For example John's Core Self with Lucy's Core Self

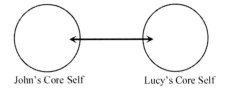

John's Core Self   Lucy's Core Self

The interaction between Lucy and John is mutually beneficial, supportive, harmonious and enjoyable and is carried out with integrity and honesty.

2. The interaction of one Ego with another's Core Self

For example the Ego of John with the Core Self of Lucy or vice versa

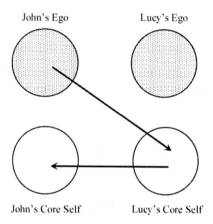

In this particular example none of Lucy's Ego parts are triggered. Lucy stays centred, peaceful, in her power and she responds from that place and reaches John's Core Self.

3. The Interaction of one Ego with another Ego

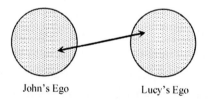

For example an Ego part of John (e.g. the 'I am not good enough'-part) activates and interacts with an Ego part of Lucy (e.g. the 'nobody cares about me'-part), playing out a well-established dance.

Quite often in Ego–Ego interactions the issue of one person triggers and dovetails with a particular issue of another person and the two inadvertently induce each other to become entrenched in their respective unhelpful perspectives.

For example Lucy has an issue with boundaries. John has an

issue with rejection. John wants to spend time with Lucy. Lucy is keen to read her new book, which she is totally immersed in. John sees his request not being met with enthusiasm as a rejection. Lucy feels harassed and pressurised. Both are offended and hurt and they may remain in that state until something (e.g. something they hear or see) causes them to change their focus. Alternatively one or both may purposefully opt to view the situation differently or they may discuss their grievances and gain a better understanding of their own and/or each other's issue.

e) With regard to our unconscious Ego parts, different scenarios are possible:

A particular Ego part may lie **dormant** or inactive. Yet although the dormant part has no impact on our present moment, it is there in the background, available to be activated at any time.

It may be difficult to discover a dormant Ego part, unless we are particularly alert, keen observers of our thoughts and what catches our attention. However, it is not crucial to ferret out any unconscious part because sooner or later something will activate this part and our emotions will make us aware of it.

Or a particular Ego part may become **activated** by an external stimulus such as the action or communication of another or a specific incident or situation. Our feelings of discomfort or unease will alert us when an Ego aspect is asserting itself.

When an unconscious Ego part has become **activated**, we have several options:

o We allow, without reflective thoughts, the activated part to govern our response to our 'negative' experience such as hurt, fury, depression or sadness. This may involve verbal or physical attack in retaliation for the perceived offence or it may involve blaming ourselves or others or retreating into self-pity or any other internal talk or throwing ourselves into some activity or any other form of avoidance. In other words, we react to the incident outwardly or inwardly. In doing so we remain unaware of the triggered part or perspective.

o We may, without probing, become aware of an unhelpful perspective or notion and yet be reluctant to disengage the dysfunctional viewpoint.

o We process our 'negative' feelings to discover an unconscious, detrimental notion, perspective or attitude making up this particular ego aspect and we change it.

o We may just stay with our uncomfortable feelings and experience them, without engaging in the triggering thoughts. Some insights or understanding may spontaneously emerge.

o We use our 'negative' feelings as a cue that our present perspective and our judgement of the 'offending' incident is off-course with our deeper truth or Essence. Having acknowledged ourselves as the sole creators of all our experiences we proactively intervene and adopt a perspective which is more on course with our Core Self. We deliberately decide how we intend to experience this situation and we choose an attitude which is of benefit to one and all.

We may always deliberately override a particular Ego aspect when it becomes active. If we choose this option every time a 'negative' feeling alerts us that an Ego perspective has surfaced, then we gradually erode all our Ego aspects. Yet at some stage of our development our Ego aspects serve their purpose.

2.4 The relevance of our adopted Ego parts and our choices with regard to them

a) The role of our Ego aspects:

In the comparison of the Ego with the Core Self, the Ego may appear the less favourable way of functioning. Yet the Ego has its role and purpose.

For one the drama, the up and down, the roller-coaster of emotions and associated experiences, sponsored by our Ego parts, may suit us at a certain stage in our life. It provides a multitude of different experiences and learning until it stops being desirable and of value.

The Ego parts are the fruits of our past choices and they were created from the understanding we had then. Nonetheless, they are of value now for at least two reasons:

o Without experiencing some of the Ego qualities such as turmoil, depression, confusion and limitation we would not fully appreciate and experience Core Self qualities such as peace, elation, clarity and freedom.
o The processing of our Ego aspects provides us with stepping-stones to a better understanding, clarity and experiential knowing. The platform of not-knowing allows us to access new understanding and insights if we are prepared to explore, to confront and to reflect. If there was not a place of not-knowing, we could not arrive at a place of understanding and knowing.

However, there comes a time when some or all the Ego aspects have outlived their function, when we have experienced enough restrictions, enough chaos, enough pain. Then it is time to move past our limitations into a more complete understanding and clarity and to connect more prominently with our Core Self.

So what effect has the reduction of our Ego parts on our overall well-being?

b) Transformation and reduction of our Ego parts and increasing the prominence of our Core Self aspect is about moving:

from	to
partial unconsciousness, not being fully aware	becoming fully conscious and aware of all of ourselves
our adopted, invented, fictional Self	our true, real, authentic Self
fragmentation, separation and isolation	intimacy, unity, oneness
not working coherently and purpose-fully together	operating coherently, harmoniously and deliberately
the focus and attention being diffuse or scattered and at times being channelled in opposing directions	our focus, attention and energy being channelled in the direction of our chosen priorities and intentions
contradiction and inconsistency between actions, communications and thoughts.	communications, thoughts and actions all being consistent with each other and the selected priorities
meeting with limitations, conflict, turmoil, suffering, frustrations, disappointments, guilt and all manner of undesirable emotions and experiences	being the embodiment of peace, freedom, power, joy, fulfilment, exhilaration
our energy being drained and dispersed by our parts engaging in various, haphazard and often opposing undertakings, by inner conflict, unrest, a high consumption of emotional energy, and by lack of focus	our energy and use of time being channelled with maximum efficiency and effectiveness towards our priori-ties and intentions
the pursuit of our goals being hampered, even jeopardised or sabotaged by inner struggles, opposi-tion of parts and counterproductive actions, by inconsistency and lack of clarity	the pursuit of our goal being conducted with the joint forces of thoughts, words and actions, with a minimum of obstacles (with each obstacle serving as a stepping-stone towards the goal) and with maximum ease, efficiency and effectiveness

Our overall progression or evolution proceeds from a high degree of disunity to complete unity in our being. We evolve from a great number of disjointed, counterproductive fragments to all our parts working in unison with our Core Self.

Where we are on this overall progression is indicated by how far we have moved towards the Core Self's way of being. To give a few examples, the degree of progression from a large number of Ego parts to major Core Self integration is indicated by:

Where our priorities lie;
To what degree we take responsibility i.e. how many of our choices we own;
What we focus on and pay attention to;
How deeply we know ourselves;
The degree to which our attention and focus is in the present;
The degree to which we experience freedom, peace, fulfilment and joy.

c) Why the transformation of our Ego parts is so worthwhile for us and such a blessing to others:

This is illustrated with the aid of the following diagrams. Please note that the diagrm below is not reflecting the physical location or the relative volume of our respective Ego parts and our Authentic or Core Self, but it is intended to demonstrate the impeding effect of a large number of Ego parts on the ease with which we and others may access our Core Self.

Ego aspects

Notions we ponder and questions we ask ourselves

Communications and interactions of others intended for our Real, Intrinsic Self

Authentic Self

do not reach our Essence. We miss out on the beneficial response and wisdom of our innate knowing.

bounce off without being truly received by our Authentic Self. Our response is governed by that 'triggered' Ego part.

The diagram is meant to pictorially convey that a multitude of Ego parts considerably impairs access to our wise Authentic Self. When we are looking for solutions or seeking greater clarity and understanding, then a huge prominence of Ego aspects makes it much more difficult to procure the discerning, supportive, enriching input from our Core Self. Instead, most likely we encounter one or several of our Ego aspects and receive a less than beneficial, fear-sponsored perspective or notion. Equally, when others communicate or interact with us they most likely meet one or more of our Ego aspects and the response they receive will reflect the perspective held by those 'triggered' Ego parts and they miss out on the beneficial response which our Essence has to offer.

When, however, most of our unhelpful aspects are trans-formed and in line with our Core Self, we and others gain much more easily access to our Authentic, Wise Self.

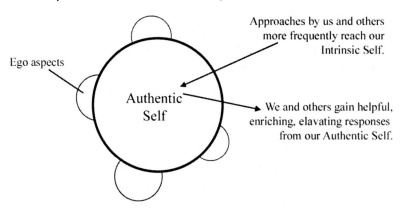

Therefore the more of our Ego parts we transform, the more frequently and easily we (and others) enjoy the tremendous benefits and exhilaration our Core Self has to offer.

d) Discovering and transforming our Ego parts by processing our negative feelings:

There are many ways to become aware of and change our restrictive, retarding Ego parts. A very effective and fast method is the processing of our uncomfortable feelings as described in Part 1. In essence we go through a process as follows:

o We first become aware that we are experiencing a negative feeling.

o As soon as we realise that our body is experiencing unpleasant emotional sensations, we need to remind ourselves that this is a brilliant opportunity to discover a perspective, belief or way of being which is not serving us well and which is out of touch with who we are at our Core.

o We need to accept and own that our emotions are due to the perspective or attitude we have opted for and that the feelings we experience are not caused by the external happenings.

o The next step is to purposefully intervene and to proactively take our focus off the triggering event. Thus we deliberately disengage with the issue. If the feeling was due to a particular attachment, we need to loosen our grip on the pain-promoting attachment.

o Instead we engage with the sensations of our feelings, hear them and experience them fully until we sufficiently penetrate them. We allow them to diffuse.

o We pay attention to what realisation or understandings arise as a result of penetrating and interacting with the aroused emotion(s).

o If the unhelpful or detrimental perspective or way of being is not immediately obvious, we need to dig a little deeper by way of a series of questions, asking ourselves repeatedly "Why is this making me feeling such and such?" and then paying attention to what we hear ourselves saying. We need to pursue this line of questioning until we have uncovered the core or most central issue. This requires total honesty and courage. Sometimes we find that what we find so hurtful in others is something we are doing ourselves.

o For this exploration to be fruitful, it must be undertaken when we are in a calm, centred place. When in the midst of emotional turmoil, our clarity and vision is considerably diminished and we most likely do not have access to the understanding available to us. We probably only gather more unhelpful thoughts.

o The exploration may be carried out immediately, if circumstances allow us to or later, when we have some quiet,
uninterrupted time.

o Once we have discovered the root of our uncomfortable
feelings, we need to act upon the procured insight and adopt
a more beneficial perspective, attitude or way of being. We
may use our body sensations as a guide to discover the most
beneficial, elating, powerful notion or way of being available
to us. In some instances it may be helpful to undertake an
outer action such as sharing our issue with the other(s)
involved or establishing some boundaries. However, for this
action to effect beneficial outcomes, it must come from a
calm, uncharged place and be offered in a clear and caring
manner.

o The newly adopted perspective needs to be pursued,
reinforced and strengthened on an ongoing basis in order to
erode the outdated notion and to nurture the new one, until
the newly adopted one becomes our default viewpoint or
belief. Our feelings will always let us know when we have
slipped back into the obsolete, disadvantageous perspective.

Most of our parts or ways of being evolve gradually or in stages
and not in a single jump. For example, over time, with each
conscious decision and act of accepting ourselves, we learn to
accept ourselves more fully until eventually we have reached a
stage where we are accepting all of ourselves on a permanent
basis. However, some perspectives or ways of being may change
instantaneously.

Each detrimental Ego aspect that we become aware of and
change into a more advantageous one not only stops us from
experiencing negative emotions in situations which previously
caused that particular aspect to be activated, but it also has an
effect on the whole of our being. Many of our relationships and
interactions become more satisfactory. Our outlook and way of
being improves; we become more at ease, freer, more confident
and light-hearted.

e) The mirror method:

Another fast and powerful way to ferret out our impeding Ego aspects is by using everything and anything that catches our attention to inform us about ourselves. In this way the 'outside' world may serve as a 'mirror' for our 'inner' world.

Our 'mirror' shows us our orientation, our way of being, the dynamic between our different parts and the happenings in our internal world. It enables us to discover our unconscious misconceptions, erroneous thoughts, unhelpful behaviour, our unconscious attitudes and intentions, and all those aspects of ourselves that we judge negatively and have disowned. Everything that we notice out there or that is speaking to us, is showing us something about ourselves. It is just a question of how much we allow ourselves to see and whether we want to act on what we discover.

The mirror method is similar to processing our negative emotions in that unpleasant emotions may be involved and it may also require that we confront something within ourselves that we judge negatively. However, the mirror process is also applicable when we experience neutral or even positive emotions. In that respect it is a more comprehensive or widely applicable method to access our unconscious data; everything may be used for this purpose and the method is only limited by how much we allow ourselves to see. Yet with this method we do not necessarily have our emotions to prompt us and we have to be more proactive and observe with acute and astute attention. We have to keep ourselves alert and open to what is reflected in front of us.

Here are a few examples to illustrate the mirror concept:

o I know quite a few people who frequently and freely dish out severe criticism. Yet they themselves react strongly, with great anger and hurt, to perceived criticism or even to mere observations.

There is a difference between criticism and observation: an

observation is a declaration of what is so, without any value or judgement of good or bad attached. When criticising something we judge it negatively.

o A relative of mine complained to me bitterly that other relatives did not leave her be, who she wanted to be. Yet she herself had very strong ideas about how others should behave and what they should do, or not do, and voiced her opinions forcefully. She did not connect what she felt done to her with being something she was doing herself.

o At a party I overheard a group of women deploring the actions of the boyfriend of another woman. I caught myself judging them negatively for it and thus emulating their behaviour. They acted as a mirror for my own tendency.

o A friend of mine was unsuccessfully seeking intimacy with his girlfriend. Yet, he was very defensive and rebuffing in his interactions with her and thus greatly hindering closeness. He projected his lack of openness and availability out there onto her.

o Another friend of mine was quite inflexible with respect to considering alternatives or making any changes. Yet she constantly accused her partner of being inflexible. She noticed out there was what she was doing herself.

o I frequently catch myself saying something to somebody else, which applies to me e.g. 'You are not hearing, what I am saying' or 'You are not paying attention'. Invariably it means that I am not paying attention or that I am not hearing. Thus I learned to listen carefully to what I am saying to others, especially when in an emotionally charged state.

o Some of what we see out there may serve either as a model for an attitude, quality aspect or way of behaving we might want to adopt, or as a model for something we may want to avoid or decide not to do or be.

o The 'mirror' does not necessarily reflect for example the quality to the same degree as the quality in us. We also may exhibit this quality or behaviour in quite a different aspect of our life. For example, we notice a gross act of betrayal out there, which may be a 'mirror' for a less prominent occurrence of us betraying ourselves. We may act contrary to what we know would be in our best interests e.g. we may abuse our body with harmful food or drinks and thus undermine the beneficial activities of our body. This is then mirrored in the gross transgression we observe being committed out there and we feel scornful and derisive.

Exploring the source of our indignation we would meet full-on the abuse of our body. This does not preclude that what we notice does not require some outer action e.g. the disclosure of the betrayal or supporting the betrayed. However, if we are reacting strongly and judge the incident negatively, then there is always something for us to ferret out and address within ourselves. If this were not the case, then we would just register the occurrence and calmly, without our emotions being engaged, undertake the appropriate, beneficial actions. Incidentally, this is an example where the Process method and the Mirror method overlap.

What the mirror may show us and how it is used:

o We notice other people's characteristics or ways of being:

If somebody seems to be domineering, short-tempered, deceitful, close-minded, aggressive, fretful or a perfectionist and it meets our disapproval, then we need to ask ourselves: Why does this stand out for me? What does this tell me about me? Do I think or act like that?

If we have become aware, through what has been mirrored to us, that we are not satisfied with the extent to which we are expressing a particular quality e.g. honesty, empathy, acceptance, diligence etc., then we can undertake steps to express this quality more frequently or to a higher degree. This may require repeated reinforcement of our decision, a strong intention and constant reminders to following our decision through. Yet what we observe out there will remind us of our tendencies and bring us back to our decision.

o We witness the relationships between others and/or our relationships with others:

How others interact with us and each other and the quality and dynamic of these relationships display to us a particular dynamic going on within us. It can demonstrate to us how we treat ourselves and others, or show the degree of intimacy we have with ourselves.

If we do not immediately get a sense what the observed relationship pattern is illustrating, we might want to 'sit' with some of the following questions in some quiet moments: What is this interaction, that gets my attention, showing me? What dynamic within myself is displayed out there? In what way do I treat myself or others like this?

Observing and exploring relationship dynamics is an extremely powerful way to become more intimate with ourselves.

o We watch situations, events, happenings:

What is happening out there may give us an indication of what is going on within us. To me it is infinitely fascinating and interesting to see something being so clearly displayed in front of me and to make the connection as to how it applies to some of my aspects. It never fails to amaze and excite me.

In order to get a better handle on what is being played out in front of us, if it doesn't become immediately clear, it might be helpful to ask ourselves: What is the essence of this event, that gets my attention? What in me is this representing? In what area of my inner world is this dynamic happening?

o We pay attention to what we say to others.

The close observation of our comments, requests or questions may prove highly revealing. We may surprise ourselves by the choice of words or the content of our message and we may wonder where it came from. Some deep truth or revelation may emerge from a casual, uncensored remark. Equally, we may find, on closer inspection, that what we pronounce to others, is something that applies to us equally and would serve us well to take note of.

Once we have trained ourselves to listen carefully to what we are saying, realisations accumulate hard and fast. There was a time, when I became almost reluctant to say anything, because everything I was pointing out applied to me and I was ready for a break from awareness.

o We deliberately observe our own internal dialogue.

This dialogue may be verbal or non-verbal, in the form of images, moods or sensations. Becoming a keen and alert observer of our internal conversation can bring to light our often semi-conscious preoccupations, our quarrels, some quite unexpected judgements, tendencies or anxieties, our unexpressed or unacknowledged fantasies and dreams. Once in the daylight of our conscious awareness we may adopt different priorities or focus our mind on subject matters of our conscious choosing.

o We witness the conversations of others with us and between others.

Notwithstanding what others intend to convey, their communications may bring us unexpected answers, sudden realisations or generally serve to increase our awareness and reduce our unconscious or non-conscious data.

In short: what we hear or see will show us some perspective, quality or behaviour we have either adopted or we have neglected to promote. Having become aware of this we are then in a position to make desirable changes.

What is required to work with what the mirror shows us:

It may require a huge amount of willingness and intent to open ourselves to noticing and acknowledging our detrimental, limiting ideas, beliefs, perspectives. We close ourselves to 'seeing' what there is to see when our sense of self-worth is quite fragile and we unconsciously protect it with huge, powerful defences. We defend ourselves with the notion that we are misunderstood, misjudged, that part of us or all of us is rejected, that our ability or competence is questioned, or the assumption that we are attacked in any other number of ways.

However, not facing a particular part of ourselves has as a consequence that we close ourselves to getting to know ourselves better, that the unhelpful part stays with us as it is and we cannot change it and that it diminishes our experience of freedom and peace.

Letting the outside inform us about ourselves is a fascinating, exciting, infinitely interesting undertaking. We get endless surprises, as many surprises and insights as we can leave ourselves open to. In addition the journey of discovery leads us to a much freer, more meaningful and satisfactory life, a life more on a par with our Essence.

In this chapter I have mentioned two ways of reducing our unconscious Ego elements. Applying the Process and/or the Mirror method we not only get to know ourselves better, but more importantly, we lessen the amount of our Ego components and we increase the prominence of our Core way of being. In other words, we further the experience of more of our Core qualities such as peace, joy, beauty and freedom in our daily life.

Another way to promote fulfilment, passion, joy, ease and harmony in our life is to proactively target the predominance of our Core Self in our Being. By deliberately reaching for and accessing our Core Self and purposefully spending more time on course with our Essence, we boost our average share of feeling happy, content and peaceful and equally reduce the amount of time we spend in various degrees of discomfort. In those moments, when we manage to deeply connect with our Core Self, our Ego parts are completely silenced. Moreover if, whilst in the midst of uncomfortable feelings, we manage to reach out to and align with our Core Self, we experience instantly a shift in our thoughts and feelings. Without having to search for a more helpful perspective, we instantly view the situation or incident differently; we are immediately immersed in a sea of beneficial, good-feeling perspectives.

For all those reasons and many more it is immensely advantageous and useful to actively seek out and align with our Essence. Ways of achieving this are discussed in the next part, Part 3.

Part 3

Our Core Self

3.1 Approaching a Core Self way of being

Although at times we automatically are the embodiment of who we are at our Core, there are ways to promote this way of being more proactively and deliberately. In doing so, we are able to benefit from and enjoy the beauty and exhilaration of the Core Self state more extensively and profoundly. There is no limit to the degree of satisfaction, well-being, happiness, peace and freedom this pursuit of our Core Self way of being may bring us. And this is accessible to all of us.

All methods of approaching a Core Self way of being basically involve elevating or promoting our overall energy to an increasingly higher level until we reach the energy level of our Core Self and become one with it. The greater the disparity in energy between us and the energy of our Core Self, the further removed and the more disconnected we are from our Essence. Whenever we undertake to approach our Core Self state and to connect with who we are in Essence, we decrease the gap in energy between us and the energy of our Essence. Thus, anything that promotes, elevates or increases our energy vibration serves as a tool for accessing and merging with our Core Self. There are countless ways which may achieve this. In this chapter I offer a few techniques which effectively serve this purpose.

At different times some techniques may be more appropriate and effective than others. The example methods may be used in various combinations or on their own. Again we need to be guided by our intuition. Our intense desire and intent to become more intimate and closely connected with our Core Self will guide us to what strikes a chord with us and effects the desired outcome.

Access to our Core Self is greatly eased and enhanced by a healthy, well-functioning body and mind.

a) Live healthily

Our body is the instrument with which we operate in this existence. It is the tool with which we function in the material world and connect with our non-material aspects. Thus a healthy body generally greatly eases conscious contact with our spiritual aspect.

To promote a healthy body, if it is not already functioning well, we have to attentively listen to it. It will let us know, by feelings of comfort and discomfort, resistance or elation, what it needs:

o In terms of rest, quiet time or sleep. We need to make sure we have sufficient rest and not artificially drive ourselves past periods of tiredness.

o In terms of the intake of food and drink. We need to make sure that we take in a sufficient quantity of good-quality fluid, whatever suits our body best. We also need to eat food that makes us feel well-nourished and energised and leaves us satisfied, and avoid food that deflates us, makes us feel sluggish, uncomfortable, de-energised or leaves us unsatisfied and craving.

My body lets me know quickly if something does not suit it or support it. As always, it is our choice whether we pay attention to or follow our bodily signals. Yet our body determines to a significant degree our quality of life.

o In terms of exercise, fresh air and natural light. We need a certain amount of movement, cardiovascular activity, healthy air and sunlight in a day or a week. The amount varies from person to person. We certainly benefit from exercise of some kind on a regular basis and the more fun we have the better. We can achieve a real, profound high from pursuing a sport which excites us and which we feel passionate about.

o In terms of our living and working environment. Our environment needs to be free of toxins such as unhealthy fumes, excessive noise or excessive negative radiation emitted by e.g. computers, TVs, mobile phones and certain electrical devices. It needs to contain plenty of natural light, good quality air and be pleasing to the eye and inspiring. Clutter, disorder and chaos lower our well-being.

 Our body may be more sensitive in some areas than others, but it will always let us know what supports it most effectively, if we are prepared to pay attention.

o In terms of our mental and emotional states our health is equally affected by these. When we entertain perspectives, thoughts and attitudes which are unhelpful, then our emotional and overall energy will be depressed or lowered. We may feel inferior or angry, frustrated or disappointed. Those lowered or depressed energy states we experience as sensations of discomfort and unwellness. The lowered energy also negatively impacts on our body and eventually results in various physical symptoms and illnesses. Apart from harbouring detrimental thoughts our mental state is also negatively influenced by lack of stimulation and use. We may raise our mental condition by exposing our mind to uplifting material and by reflecting and pondering on meaningful subjects. Our overall well-being is also furthered by avoiding what bores or alienates us and doing what enthuses and inspires us.

All the methods described below will improve our physical health. Yet caring for and supporting our body will assist us in the pursuit of all those other techniques. Although living healthily is not a technique as such to reach into our Core Self, it is mentioned here because it fundamentally supports all the other approaches. It is so much more difficult to initiate or maintain a connection with our Essence when we are tired, stressed or unwell. The Ego is always more prominently in the foreground under those conditions.

 One method, which does guide us towards our Core way of

being, is seeking out and engaging in what enthuses and inspires us.

b) Seek out inspiration

Anything that lifts, enthuses, brings joy, laughter or lightness serves this purpose. If we don't already know what has this effect on us, we may consider and try out a few of the suggestions below. A strong intention to find the most suitable and effective method will lead us there.

Here are just a few suggestions, which may serve the purpose of elevating our energy to a Core Self level:

o We read inspiring, uplifting poems, articles or books.
o We collect inspiring, motivating or humorous quotes and assemble or display them in a pleasing manner (maybe on cards or in a folder). Then we need to look at the reservoir of inspiring quotes frequently, especially when a positive input is particularly relevant.
o We listen to motivational or enthusing tapes or CDs.
o We listen to stirring, elating music, whenever possible.
o We dance, do yoga, tai chi or other elating moving art forms.
o We watch videos, films, programmes, which are meaningful and produce a positive shift.
o We look at and observe closely a beautiful flower, plant, picture, sculpture, garden or whatever touches and lifts us.
o We travel to inspiring locations, to hike in mountains, a forest or wood, along a river, a lake, an ocean, any magical place, or just go for a walk in the neighbourhood.
o We do activities such as gardening, creating something beautiful or amusing, painting, cooking, taking pictures, whatever we love doing.
o We carry out a sport or physical activity, which excites and moves us to a more calm and serene plane e.g. a martial art, sky-diving, horse-riding.
o We observe or be with animals or children.

o We seek out the company of inspiring people.
o We attend an inspirational talk, workshop, course.
o We look up at the sky and watch the changing formation of clouds; that works well for me.

It generally serves us well to practise one or more of the above to support ourselves with regular positive inputs, but it is especially crucial to use those tools when we feel deflated, out of sorts or out of balance or feel particularly disconnected. Yet it is always worthwhile to seek out what inspires us and promotes joy, exhilaration, serenity and peace and to avoid what pulls us down, discourages and dampens our spirit. We may purposefully assemble an arsenal of moments of immense elation and joy or of profound peace. We then add to this arsenal by frequently reactivating those experiences, by recalling the memory of those moments or by seeking out whatever evoked the original experience. In purposefully gathering and cultivating experiences of deep joy and exhilaration, we raise our overall energy to an elevated platform. This raised platform enables us to reach more readily and more deeply into our Essence and merge with it.

In a similar manner to this method, we are propelled towards our Core Self way of being, when we do what excites us or what enthrals us with enthusiasm and passion.

c) Follow our excitement and passion

When we do something with genuine joy, eagerness and zest, we automatically function as one with our Essence. We bring meaning and fulfilment into our life. The more of our waking time we engage in elevating, enthusing activities, the more our overall being benefits from it.

To get to this place, we may need to:

o Find out what that activity is for us. Again our keen desire will lead us to what captures our interest and enthusiasm. For example

- We may do visualisation exercises such as visualising and noting down what our most perfect, ideal day or week would be. What would we be doing? What features most prominently? This may give us a clue as to the essence of what inspires us.
- Feelings of comfort, ease, elation in our body guide us to what is of benefit to us and feelings of resistance or dread in our body show us, what we need to avoid.
- We may scan our life, especially our childhood, for what we used to like or for occasions and moments when we carried out something with passion, joy and enthusiasm.
- We may just observe carefully what we are drawn to, what we enjoy doing.

o Once we know what kindles our fire, we need to explore ways of making it a major part of our life. We may have to be creative or 'think outside the box' to find a way. We may also have to be focused, determined or courageous, because obstacles, objections or resistance may present themselves, from others and from within ourselves. We may have to move outside of our comfort zone. Some upheaval or quite a number of changes may be involved. Of course, none of this may be the case, and it may be all done in convenient and gentle stages. However, should a considerable effort and inconvenience be necessary, then the continuous elation, joy and fulfilment we experience, once we have arrived, will make any temporary discomfort and hardship very much worthwhile.

To launch ourselves out of the Ego state and into the Core Self or Spirit state we may very effectively use what I call 'shifters'.

d) Use 'shifters'

As 'shifters' I define anything that produces an instant and significant positive shift in our attitude, perception, mood or way of being.

There is a whole range of tools, which may have this effect:

1. We may remind ourselves:
   'I opt for peace here.'
   'My intention is harmony.'
   'I always have a choice.'
   'I may change my mind at any time.'
   'I create the meaning here.'
   'I am not doing that any more.'
   'I intend to be who I wish to be, and **not** who I presently think I am.'
   'I choose to be, e.g., patient, honest, graceful, accepting.'
   'I can't lose. I may gain from this.'
   'I do not make anything a necessity; I make everything a choice.'
   'It's not **against** me, it's **for** them.'
   'I am so, so lucky.'
   'Life is magnificent.'

2. We may ask ourselves the question:
   'Is this who I am?'
   'What would my Core Self do now?'
   'What would my wise (peaceful, liberated, courageous, confident, free) Self do now?'
   'What would I do if I had a higher perspective?'
   'What would I do if I had all the answers?'
   'What is my contribution to this situation?'
   'Is fear, guilt, regret etc. helpful here?'
   'Am I doing what I would choose to do, where I would choose to do it and with whom?'
   'Am I contributing or hindering?'
   'Am I expanding or contracting?'
   'Am I of benefit or detriment?'

3. We may make the decision:
  - To be grateful for, appreciate and value a particular situation or interaction for what we may gain from it.
  - To seek out the benefit of something we initially judged as unwelcome or negative.
  - To no longer hold on to our resentment, anger, disappointment, frustration; to embrace the willingness to simply let go.
  - To forgive a particular incident – we no longer hold on to our sense of being wronged, treated unfairly, being misjudged – and to let go of our desire for revenge or retaliation. Thus we release a huge burden from our shoulders. This is of great benefit to the person doing the forgiving as well as to the person being forgiven.
  - To consciously focus on the Core Self of the other, which has essentially the same core quality as ours.

4. We may change our perspective:
  - We may opt for the perspective that if somebody acts unreasonably, offensively, disrespectfully, aggressively, it is his/her fear or misunderstanding speaking or acting and not his/her True Self. Instead of focusing on the attack, anger or insult we may empathise with the fear, confusion or pain that person is experiencing, or we may seek to relate to the Authentic Self of that person rather than the acting-out Ego. We may also remind ourselves that we sometimes act unreasonably or in an unhelpful manner and therefore must allow others to do the same.
  - We may remind ourselves that nothing matters unless we make it matter. Then we need to examine why we made that particular occurrence matter.
  - We may decide not to judge something as failure, but to see it as a neutral event, which may serve as

feedback, as a brilliant opportunity to gain insights and understanding and to learn what we need to know for the next step. Instead of failure, we view the event or situation as a welcome stepping-stone towards our future success.

- We may adopt the perspective that 'I am not incompetent. Just the task at hand and I are a mismatch.' We may want to explore if we can make it a match. In any case, if we fail at something it does not mean that we are useless. It just means that it hasn't worked out yet.
- We become aware of and see the perfection in everything. Everything is a brilliant opportunity to grow, evolve, become wiser, more peaceful, freer, more accepting, compassionate.
- We reframe 'I can't' into 'I won't'; this shifts our stance from a helpless victim to an active creator. Likewise to reframe 'I should ...' into 'I choose to ...' reminds us that we have a choice and affirms us as creators rather than choice-less victims.

We may also approach our Core Self by purposefully and deliberately becoming more open and inclusive, by increasingly encompassing more of the universe.

e) Open up, expand and become more inclusive

We may open ourselves wide:

o To new experiences and ways of being;
o To changing our perspective and seeing things differently;
o To readily changing our mind i.e. changing the content of our mind, whenever an idea, notion, belief is not working for us, replacing the non-functional idea with a new one;
o To giving and receiving good-will and love in abundance;
o To becoming all-accepting, tolerant, gracious;
o To seeing all there is to see;

o To experiencing, sensing and connecting with our Essence;
o To experiencing the universe and all it has to offer.

We may increasingly embrace and then let go with enthusiasm:
o Our fears, doubts, feelings of guilt, shame, resentment, anger, disappointment etc.
o All that we judge negatively in ourselves and in others.
o All our projections.

We expand, when we:
o Experiment and become adventurous, pushing boundaries and moving past our comfort zone.
o Are flexible, embracing changes openly and enthusiastically.
o Enlarge our perspectives, exploring new horizons, casting our awareness further afield.

Another way of moving more closely into our Core way of being is by becoming independent of our needs.

f) Transcend our needs and attachments

Needs are here defined as something we require in order to be at peace and content.

Some of the deep-seated, fundamental needs, common to many of us, are the need to be accepted (a prominent need; acceptance is the highest form of love), to be paid attention to, to be heard and understood, to be recognised and seen, to have worth, to be valued and appreciated, to be intimate or connected, to be free and autonomous, to be safe, for our life to have purpose and meaning.

Other needs and requirements may involve others being or behaving in a certain way e.g. being honest, courteous, reliable, or others giving a particular kind of support, or something, e.g. a situation or environment, being a certain way.

Needs, as defined here, are generally disempowering and limiting, because they cause us to be dependent on somebody or something for our peace and happiness. When we loosen the grip of our needs, we start reclaiming our power and become more akin to our Core Self, who essentially has no needs.

To transcend a need we have to first become aware that we have a particular need e.g. the need to be accepted. It is amazing how often we do not realise that we have a particular under-lying, deep-rooted yearning.

Once we are conscious of a need, we have to acknowledge, own and appreciate it. Denying a need, because we despise our dependence, closes the door to moving past it and drives the need underground.

We may discover some of our unaware needs as part of the Process or Mirror method. Needs may occur in layers. We may discover a more fundamental need underneath a more superfi-cial need, e.g. the need to be included in a group activity may have at its core the need to be accepted or the need to feel connected or a need for intimacy. In this case we may primarily address the core need and the superficial need will automatic-ally become obsolete.

Once we are aware of a particular need or attachment, we may deal with it in a variety of ways:

o We may cater for our needs, where this is helpful and not in conflict with our overall priorities, by doing whatever is necessary to achieve the desired.

o We give ourselves (and others) that which we long to receive from others. For example, if we crave acceptance from certain people (as I did) we endeavour to accept ourselves (and others) to an increasingly higher degree. This has a twofold effect. Firstly, this particular need will gradually lessen until it eventually disappears altogether. Secondly, we will start to receive that which we previously so craved and we now no longer depend on.

o We may decide to gradually let go of a specific requirement. This does not mean that we pretend that it no longer exists. Equally, releasing our attachment for something to occur or be a particular way does not imply that we let go of our intention to have something. However, in both cases it does mean that we lessen our investment in that intense yearning. We elevate it into a preference. Promoting a need into a preference takes the urgency and anxiety out of it. We are no longer heavily tied to the outcome and are therefore more relaxed and at ease.

In this context I want to address the needs of other. It is excellent practice to accommodate each other's needs, wherever this is possible without impeding our own evolution or the evolution of others. Responding to somebody else's request, however, must not interfere with responding to the callings of our own Essence. For our benefit, peace and forward movement we always need to act on the aspirations of our Essence in favour of pandering to the demands of our or another's Ego.

In addition, providing for the other, what they think they need, is not always in their highest interest. 'Helping' another might stop the other from acquiring or consolidating a particular skill or quality or impede his or her progress in some other way. We may ascertain through our body response of ease or unease whether a particular intervention is supporting the Ego or the Essence of another.

So, in what way does lessening the grip of our needs move us closer to our Core Self? Need spells dependence, restrictions and disempowerment, all the hallmarks of the Ego. Negative emotions such as fear, worry, insecurity, grief or disappointment, evoked in the wake of needs, underpin this. All of this translates into our emotional and overall energy being dampened or demoted. However, elevating our needs into preferences, or transcending them, promotes our energy to a level more akin to our Core Self.

The next method works in a somewhat similar way to the one just discussed. It involves taking responsibility for everything that is in our life. In doing so we lay claim to our full inner power and freedom and thus we function akin to our Essence.

g) Take responsibility

When we take responsibility we own our choices and whatever is in our life; we are accountable and in charge. We adopt the creator role, where we are at the cause of whatever we encounter, in favour of the victim role, where we are at the effect or mercy of events. So, what are we responsible for?

We ARE responsible for the following:

o We are responsible for all our choices. We are the owners of every action we do, every word we say and every thought we think. We are the perceiver and definer of every condition.

 We are responsible for our thoughts, beliefs, judgements, viewpoints, the meaning we give something and the perception we opt for. Adopting somebody else's belief or notion does not relieve us of the responsibility for our choice; we are still choosing. Responsibility is an intrinsic aspect of choice and free will. That we have a choice is given. We do not have a choice about having a choice. However, we may choose consciously or unconsciously, with awareness or without awareness. If we choose without awareness, we may think that we did not make a choice. Nonetheless, we are still responsible for our unconscious choices.

 We are responsible for how we experience a particular situation, incident or comment, since we are responsible for the meaning or interpretation we have chosen and the meaning we have adopted generates our feelings and experience.

o We are responsible for our communications. Therefore, we may consider and assess before we speak: What is my motive? From which place does my comment or request come? Does it come from a place of fear or good-will? What will the consequences be? (Granted, others are responsible for the meaning they give with respect to what we share, but that does not relinquish our responsibility for what we radiate out into the world.) Are we expressing ourselves with care, sensitivity and consideration? Is what we are communicating helping or hindering? Is it lifting or dampening the spirits of others? Is it liberating or limiting? Is it prone to invite hurt (bearing in mind that nobody can hurt us unless we make it so) or is it promoting healing? We are responsible for deliberating this with due consideration. However, we are also responsible to ourselves. We owe it to ourselves to be true to our Essence, to our convictions and our callings. It would be irresponsible to deny a fundamental part of ourselves in order to cater for somebody else's Ego.

o It is our responsibility to make crystal clear to the other what precisely we mean by our message or communication, so that there are no misunderstandings or misconceptions

about what we were attempting to convey.

The message we send across to the other is shaped by our conditioning and understanding. The history, character and reality of the receiver mould the message into its own specific shape. Thus there may be a discrepancy between the two interpretations and the message received may not be a carbon-copy duplicate of the message sent.

Therefore, there is a need and also a responsibility to ensure that the receiver of our communication has a close enough duplicate of what we were endeavouring to convey.

o We are responsible for not allowing ourselves to be coerced, manipulated or controlled by somebody else's Ego (the Core Self does not attempt to control and manipulate). We need to resist responding to somebody not taking responsibility and blaming us for his/her choices. Should we be in agreement with the other we would inappropriately assume responsibility for that person. In my understanding it is grossly patronising, limiting and debilitating to take responsibility for another mature sentient being.

What we **ARE NOT** responsible for are the viewpoints, beliefs or attitudes and thus the experiences of others. We may be able to assist others to adopt an understanding or perspective which is to their benefit rather than their detriment, or to make choices which bring about the experiences they are seeking. However, after we have attempted to convey to somebody the benefit of our understanding, we must resist from interfering in his/her choice. It can be quite difficult, even heart-wrenching (at least until we adopt a higher perspective) to stand by and allow others, especially those close to us, to make and carry out choices which we think are not to their advantage and which may bring temporary discomfort or suffering. However, the right to free will and choice is paramount and must be honoured.

In essence:

When others communicate with us, they present us with a glimpse of their inner world, with a slice of their opinions, their understanding or their reality. And the communication is their responsibility and concern. What we do with the communication, what meaning we give it, how we respond to it, whether we ensure we have understood it correctly or not, how we deal with any emotions it may have triggered, all of this is our concern and responsibility. When we assume responsibility we know that our choice determines whether we are empowered or disempowered, whether we gain or seem to lose as a result of the communication.

When we take responsibility we are also considerate. We own our negative emotions and hence we do not feel the need to express our emotions outwards. In diffusing our low energy emotions privately, we do not potentially affect others negatively.

Sometimes it proves necessary to enlighten the other person of how something has affected us and/or we may want to suggest or request a different behaviour for the future.

However, we do not depend, for our peace and ease, on the other person to appreciate the effect of their action, nor do we depend on them for making any changes in their behaviour or thinking.

Responsibility entails owning what is in our life:

o Chances are that we had a considerable part in creating a particular interaction or incident.
o Even if we are not directly involved in creating what we encounter, any occurrence or situation offers a whole range of choices. We at least choose our perspective or attitude and in doing so we choose how we experience the incident and we decide what we line up by way of future encounters and experiences.
o When we become the sole cause of everything we experience, then we place ourselves in full charge of our life.

Assuming ownership for all aspects of our life moves us into our innate power and freedom, which is the essence of our Core Self. Thus, through accepting ever greater responsibility we unite increasingly more profoundly and completely with our Essence.

Another way to advance progressively more fully into the heart of our Core Self is by becoming increasingly more conscious and aware.

h) Become evermore aware and conscious

Pursuit of awareness is a powerful key to all our non-conscious parts; it facilitates access to all that we have forgotten or do not realise in the here and now. It is the path of our unconscious elements into consciousness and thus a door to our Essence which is the embodiment of awareness and absolute consciousness. The more aware we become, the more closely we approach our Core way of being.

Awareness builds on itself. It starts with a spark of awareness and then exponentially increases. Awareness develops like an avalanche. Once we have had our first glimpses of realisations or insights, awareness takes off and adds to itself to an ever-increasing extent.

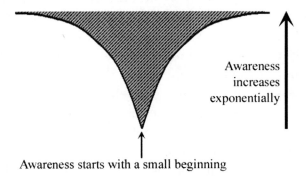

Awareness
increases
exponentially

Awareness starts with a small beginning

Awareness is increased by most, if not all the other methods discussed in this chapter. Certainly discovering and transforming our less than helpful aspects increases awareness. Cultivating periods of stillness advances insights and understanding. Reaching towards our Core Self has the same effect, as does immersing ourselves in inspiring material, promoting Core Self qualities, following our excitement or striving to be inclusive or expansive. However, awareness may be specifically targeted by a resolute intention to see all there is to see.

We may increase our awareness by observing closely, with alert attention, our thoughts, our perspectives, our attitude, our way of being, our behaviour, and by noticing what we say and what others say. In addition we may reflect on what we have observed and ask ourselves: Why am I feeling this? What is the underlying issue? What am I being here? Why am I being this? Why am I thinking this? What does this mean? Why am I saying this? Does this apply to me? Why is this happening? What is the dynamic involved? What is the underlying perception or attitude involved here?

It is also useful to record our insights and understanding in some form e.g. in a diary or book, because otherwise they may easily slip out of awareness. Once we have recorded an insight we keep hold of it to a certain degree and we can revisit it repeatedly and thus integrate it more substantially into our Being.

We may also promote awareness by being acutely present. We are not in the past or in the future or somewhere else or engaged in thoughts. When we are not entertaining thoughts, we are out of the Ego state, which consists of thoughts. When we are out of the Ego state and in the here and now, we have easy access to our Core Self. Therefore, being fully present and aware allows us to experience the most elevating qualities and sublime energy of our Core Self. This is the goal of all the techniques offered in Part 3.

The following method is quite similar to the use of awareness. It may even be seen as the same, and in essence it is. However, it may be viewed from a slightly different perspective and is thus for clarity separated out.

i) Increase our understanding and clarity and access our innate knowing

With this method we approach our Core Self increasingly more closely, because our Core Self is total clarity and understanding.

There are different levels of learning, understanding and knowing. These levels range from short- and long-term memory to an intellectual understanding and then more profoundly towards a fuller integration into our reality. The range of understanding and clarity ends with deep inner knowing, integrated without a flicker of a doubt, into our DNA and the Essence of our Being.

Our deeper levels of understanding do not require proof or scientific evidence. This kind of clarity is beyond intellectual

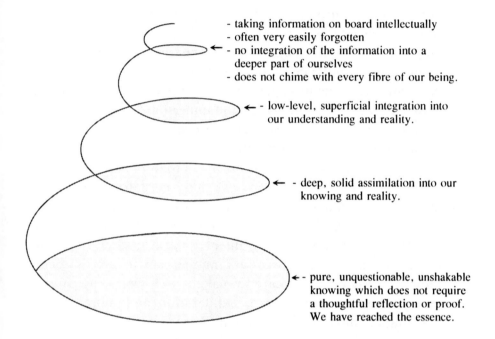

- taking information on board intellectually
- often very easily forgotten
- no integration of the information into a deeper part of ourselves
- does not chime with every fibre of our being.

- low-level, superficial integration into our understanding and reality.

- deep, solid assimilation into our knowing and reality.

- pure, unquestionable, unshakable knowing which does not require a thoughtful reflection or proof. We have reached the essence.

rationalisation or analytical reasoning. It is more a grasping and assimilating of the essence. We pervade the subject fully, from the inside out. The more deeply we understand something, the more we have hold of its essence. The essence of this knowing is already part of us. It is at the Core of our Being. In a sense we approach more closely what we already know, our own profound inner knowing.

How do we promote understanding and clarity? Processing our feelings or using the mirror method invariably furnishes us with insights and new understanding, if we are willing to see. Quiet time or stilling our thoughts may create an opening for insights to surface. Also repeatedly or intensively reflecting, ruminating or being with a subject or question may bring increased comprehension and discernment. Yet deeper levels of understanding are accessed through a more intuitive route. Our intuitions or insights seep through from more profound levels which the intellect cannot reach. So how do we foster our capacity for intuitive access to clarity? We encourage intuitive insights by a fervent intent to pursue clarity and by taking note of hunches, gut feelings and by paying attention to our sense of ease or unease. Sometimes we reach profound clarity and knowing instantaneously, without apparent prompting, in a moment of absolute certainty. However, more often we access deep understanding in stages, each act of clarity leading us more closely into the heart of clarity and understanding itself.

In all our striving to reach greater clarity and understanding we have to be honest and willing to see what there is to see, because sometimes we may feel inclined to look past something when we judge it negatively. We also need to cultivate an attitude of openness to allow new understanding in and we need to be prepared to change our mind easily. Furthermore, we need to conjure up a strong intent to gain greater clarity in order to build up the necessary momentum to get us there. However, any effort we care to make is well worth the gain of ever greater freedom, peace, exhilaration and more closely reaching the bliss of who we are in Essence.

Yet, we may shift towards the Core of our Being by becoming more at ease and at peace with what we encounter or experience.

j) The practice of non-resistance and acceptance

First of all, acceptance of an interaction, circumstance or situation does not mean that we are in agreement with it or that we support the occurrence. It means that we are at ease and at peace with the happening; we refrain from gathering energy against it.

So how does refraining from resistance and practising acceptance propel us into our Core way of being?

o For one, in resisting or opposing an offending incident or situation we invest our attention, time and energy in it; we keep it alive and nurture it. This is in contrast to what we would like to happen, namely for the inconvenient situation to improve or disappear. In addition, any negative judgement of the occurrence either feeds and strengthens an existing Ego entity or creates a new one. The net result of the above is that a) the incident and our Ego entity as a whole has gained energy and b) our well-being is diminished and our overall energy vibration is lowered.

o Conversely, acceptance frees up the energy invested in the resistance and it raises our overall energy dramatically towards the energy level of our Core Self, which in fact is the essence of acceptance. To illustrate this with a specific example: when we wholeheartedly embrace and accept a particular Ego aspect, which has been activated by an offending incident, we are instantly and powerfully catapulted **out of** the negative feelings associated with that **Ego** perspective and **into** an energy level more akin to our **Core Self.** Because this is such an effective method to shift from an active Ego entity into our Core way of being, I repeat the above statement: **When we wholeheartedly embrace the presently active Ego aspect, then we immediately shoot out of the perspective of that Ego aspect (and the uncomfortable feelings associated with it) and into the perspective or way of being of our Essence and the accompanying joy, peace and phenomenal well-being.**

o In general, when we accept or allow that which we encounter – an incident, a person or part of ourselves – we give that our highest energy and greatest gift, which is love; acceptance is the highest expression of love. Residing and operating from this high-energy state we are of maximum benefit in our actions and to all that we give attention to. Moreover, in practising acceptance we ourselves reside in a highly elevated energy state, akin to our Core Self, where we perceive only beauty and experience phenomenal harmony, exhilaration and well-being.

The route of acceptance is one of the fastest and most powerful ways to disengage Ego aspects and engage with our Core Self. Another extremely fast and effective way to erode our Ego entities and energetically align with our Essence is being appreciative.

k) The practice of appreciation

The practice of appreciation works in a similar way to the previous method. And yet it has the added capacity to raise our energy vibration to ever higher levels.

Like acceptance, appreciation and gratitude are diametrical opposites of our Ego qualities; we cannot value something and at the same time criticise or berate it, notice shortcomings or see imperfection. Thus the more we practise gratitude the more we dilute or erode our Ego aspects. However, engaging in the art of gratitude not only ensures that we are not creating any new dysfunctions or activating old ones, but more crucially, it is an extremely effective and fast way to raise our emotional and overall energy level to any extent we desire. Being truly grateful for something lifts our spirit to great heights and we align increasingly more deeply with our Core Self. Having accumulated a reservoir of gratitude through a multitude of moments of appreciation we are in a position to easily and speedily facilitate communion with our Essence.

So how do we develop an attitude of gratitude? We start with something that easily evokes our appreciation. We may appreciate anything and everything in our life. This may include people we know or even don't know, the quality of particular relationships, our state of health, features of our appearance, a particular ability or skill we have, particular animals or plants or nature in general, the state of our personal or spiritual development, what we know, our living or working environment, a particular object or possession, to name but a few. There is no limit to what we may be grateful for.

In addition to finding something that immediately pleases us we may more proactively develop an attitude of gratitude.

o We may move into gratitude for something by changing our viewpoint or perspective with respect to a particular circumstance, incident or person. Instead of focusing on what appears to be amiss we can instead focus on all that is 'positive' about it.

o We may purposefully cultivate the art of finding one or even better several aspects of value in a situation or interaction.

o We may altogether appreciate the existence and support of a benign universe.

Once we start down the route of valuing what is in our life, we find more and more things to appreciate. Appreciation attracts further appreciation and our energy rises higher and higher, in fact to any height we care to raise it. Over time the momentum of appreciation builds up a powerful arsenal of positive energy, which may serve as a platform from which we may fly even higher. And the higher our energy vibration raises, the more closely we approach the energy make-up of our Core Self. Therefore, the more we cultivate the art of being appreciative, the more we energetically line up with our Essence and live in a state of phenomenal well-being.

In addition, we may promote access to and alignment with the stillness of our Core Self by stilling our mind and silencing our thoughts.

l) The practice of stillness

There are many books available relating to this subject and many methods on offer on how to practise stillness or what sometimes is referred to as meditation. With meditation I mean any technique which facilitates the quietening of the mind.

It is not the scope of this book to describe these methods in detail or even to present a list of the various methods available. When we are willing and strongly intend to work towards a certain degree of stillness, then we will find a method which works for us.

It may be initially quite difficult to stop thinking. Yet we need to create a space in our daily routine where we endeavour to refrain from actively thinking. We need to purposefully stop all our planning, organising, remembering, worrying, investigating, deliberating etc. We need to withdraw our attention from the outer and move into our inner realm and do nothing, nothing at all and just be.

One way to get there, which works quite effectively, is focusing on our incoming and outgoing breath or repeating a word or expression continuously, until our thoughts slow down. It is also important to approach this in a relaxed manner, with great intent, but relaxed. Becoming angry, frustrated, disappointed or berating ourselves because we do not succeed is counterproductive.

The aim is to become mere observers of our interfering thoughts and not to engage with them; we notice them and then let them pass by. Eventually our thoughts will become less loud, less prominent, less attention-capturing, and we become more receptive and aware of our body or our feelings or our way of being. We may experience great calmness, a sense of ease and peace. Our perceptions or feelings may shift. We become receptive to more subtle messages. Insights, understandings or clarity may arise. Something may fall into place, ideas or solutions may emerge. We may feel great elation, joy, contentment or enthusiasm.

Those moments of stillness do not generally happen by themselves. We have to actively seek them out. This requires:

o That we make it a high enough priority, so that we make it happen.
o A strong intention and determination to carry us through to finding a suitable method and to making time, when we think we don't have the time.
o That we create time for this on a daily basis. A good time is first thing in the morning, when the brain is not very active yet.
o A certain degree of persistence and perseverance to carry us through possible difficult periods.

movement. Alternatively, we may recall the memory of a moment when we felt totally at ease and at peace or when we felt immense joy or were highly elevated, in other words, when we experienced a high energy state. Hooking into and reconnecting with that experience or similar experiences may effectively lift our emotional energy to a similar elevated level, akin to our Core energy. From this position we can easily feel the extremely exhilarating energy of our Core Self and experientially merge with it.

o Alongside advancing towards our Essence we need to enter into an internal dialogue with it. We may express our intentions, wishes or hopes or we may ask for assistance with this connection or communicate whatever is on our mind. This communication may take place on a mental or a feeling level. Alternatively, it may be expressed image-wise or sound-wise, whichever way we communicate most profoundly and with the greatest depth and intensity. Whichever means we use, we strive to interact with our Centre of love, joy, stillness and freedom by seeking it out with loving intention, by speaking to it, by giving it our utmost attention and focus and by being attentively and perceptively open to a response. The more we value and appreciate this connection with our Core Self and the more of ourselves we put into this contact and communication, the more intimate and rewarding the relationship will be.

o We need to persist in our effort to connect with our Core Self until we have received a response. This may happen immediately or some time later, maybe hours or days later. We need to pay keen attention with alert anticipation. The response may come, subtly or powerfully, in the form of:

• a feeling, such as a warm support, a sense of connectedness, profound peace, elation or any other sensation touching us positively;

• a realisation, a revelation, a sudden complete certainty, an understanding or profound, unshakable knowing;

• a sense of total security or alrightness;

• a sense of being unconditionally accepted;

- a shift in feeling about a particular situation;
- something we observe or notice in our surrounding, that 'speaks' to us, that touches us in a profound way;
- any other way, that is meaningful, revealing or illuminating to us.

We will always receive a response in time if we are earnest and persistent in our intention to reach our intrinsic Essence and we make ourselves available to a communication.

How do we know that we are not making all this up or kidding ourselves? We know by the effect this interaction has on us, by the way it touches us. If we feel uplifted, inspired, motivated by it, if we feel increased well-being, peace, freedom, joy or if we feel wiser, then we have been in contact with that part of us that personifies those qualities.

There is absolutely no doubt when we have been deeply in touch with our Spiritual Core. We will know this experientially through our body sensations and feelings, which cannot be described adequately in words; the sensations are far richer than immense elation, well-being and bliss.

o Once we have experienced a profound connection it is easier to achieve another moment of deep connectedness. For example, we may deliberately relive that experience by recalling the memory of it. Yet sometimes, for no apparent reason, without any effort on our part, in moments of tremendous grace, we will feel elated, enthused, held in high esteem or feel enveloped in total acceptance and loving, appreciative, supportive friendship. However at other times it may require some persistent, affectionate reaching out on our part, without receiving an immediate strong response. In time, with repeated, profound experiences of being in contact with our Essence it will become increasingly easier to establish a prolonged connection and to maintain it. We build up a powerful arsenal of elevated moments or a raised energy platform which enables us to tap into this exhilarated way of being more readily.

o Having entered into a deliberate relationship with our Core Self, we need to nurture, promote and deepen that relationship on a daily basis. We need to commit wholeheartedly to this connection and pursue it with passion, intensity, determination and patience and make it a high enough priority to generate sufficient time for it. Our efforts are greatly aided by a combination of some or by all the other methods described in this chapter. The amount of time and degree of fervent input we devote to it depends on how much intimacy with our Essence we desire. There is no limit to this. What we gain in our intimate, profound relationship with our Spirit aspect is beyond any description and infinitely worth every effort we care to make.

Some of the above methods work on a more ongoing and prevalent basis such as cultivating a Core Self quality or practising stillness or contacting our Core Self directly, whereas others work more short term, such as seeking out inspiration or applying 'shifters'. Yet it depends on the degree and intensity with which the method is employed. If we employ 'shifters' several times a day or whenever we catch ourselves in the Ego state, then we live basically permanently in a Core Self state.

The degree of progress towards transcending our Ego aspects and operating from the heart of our Core Self very much depends on:

o Choosing the most suitable method or methods for us.
o Applying the chosen method(s) with the greatest of intent, attention, motivation, enthusiasm and passion.
o Making it a high enough priority to devote sufficient energy and time to the application of the method on a daily basis.
o Planning and organising our daily routine so as to ensure that we integrate and accommodate the practice of the chosen method to an effective degree.
o Enlisting all the support and assistance we can raise including casting out a request for help to our Core Self

and/or the universe. We also need to avoid whatever hinders.
o Building a strong momentum which sweeps us along.
o Adopting attitudes or perspectives which propel us towards
   a particular core quality or a core state of being.
o Exercising patience and persistence, when progress appears
   to slow down or grind to a halt altogether. We do not always
   notice internal shifts and advances and things appear to be
   stationary when they are not. If we are patient enough,
   changes will occur, maybe all of a sudden, very rapidly.

The methods discussed may be applied in any combination. For
me the processing of my negative emotions and the reaching out
into the heart of my Core Self went hand in hand and one
supported the other. The contact with my Core Self afforded me
with insights, understanding and clarity, which aided the transformation of non-functioning, erroneous notions or beliefs.
Working with my emotions and uncovering my dysfunctional
ideas brought me closer to my Core Self. Thus both methods
promoted progress in the other area.

Apart from the above-mentioned methods, there are
countless other ways of approaching more closely our Core way
of being. Yet although most methods approach our high energy
Essence from different angles or by different routes, they all
involve essentially the same central feature:

All methods of accessing and merging with our Core Self
essentially involve the raising of our energy to a level more on
a par with the high energy level of our Spiritual Essence. In
other words we decrease the energy gap between us and our
Core Self. This is the key element involved in reaching
towards and merging with our Essence.

Elevation of our energy is involved in all the methods
mentioned in this chapter from seeking out inspiration,
following our excitement, using shifters, opening up and
becoming inclusive, to practising appreciation and contacting
our Core Self directly. We equally raise our energy when we

transcend our needs, take responsibility, become evermore aware, increase our clarity and access our innate knowing, practice acceptance or stillness or pursue Core qualities, because in doing so we reside in a high energy level close to our Core Self, which has no needs, is the personification of responsibility, is awareness, clarity and total knowing and is unconditional acceptance and complete stillness. In short, we mimic our Core Self and thus reside in the energy level of our Core Self.

I cannot stress highly enough that if we want to move away from our limiting Ego aspects and towards the Essence of peace, freedom and joy, we have to raise our energy by some means. We may do so by any of the methods discussed here or using any other method that works for us. However, the most immediate method of raising our energy is by seeking direct contact and communion with our Infinite Essence.

The more frequently we access our Core Self and the longer we remain aligned with It, the more we raise our overall energy level. From this elevated energy plateau:

a) It is easier to access our Spiritual Essence again *and*

b) Our Ego aspects will be less prominent and our Core aspect will be more dominant and influential in our overall being. We experience more of our Core qualities such as ease, elation and satisfaction and less discomfort and pain.

In those moments, when we are energetically aligned with our Core Self, we are enveloped and permeated with enormous exhilaration, profound peace, unmarred inner power, immense contentment and infinite joy and yet so much more than that. It cannot be described in words; we will only ever know it experientially.

3.2 Functioning and living on course with our Core Self

What will help us to align increasingly more frequently and profoundly with our Essence? We do move towards our Core or Limitless Self every time:

o We take care, nurture and support our body.
o We release some accumulated painful emotions.
o We transform a need into a preference.
o We transform an outdated aspect of ourselves.
o We change a detrimental and limiting belief, notion or idea.
o We think a beneficial thought or adopt a more helpful attitude or perspective.
o We challenge and change an unhelpful habit.
o We choose love over hate.
o We choose to forgive a perceived 'transgression' against us.
o We practise goodwill or grace.
o We choose freedom over convenience or approval.
o We become more inclusive.
o We choose not to judge
o We refrain from blaming and we make peace with what is.
o We take responsibility for our choices, thoughts, communications and actions.
o We switch to a position of trust; we foster the trust that all is intrinsically well, that we are taken care of, that the universe supports us.
o We are at peace with what we encounter and we look for the opportunities that the initially unwelcome incident presents.
o We decide to see ourselves as in charge of what we encounter

rather than the helpless, unrequired victim of a particular situation or incident.

o We choose consciously and deliberately.

o We clarify our intentions and priorities and organise our time and energy in line with what we have decided.

o We are focused in the present.

o We follow our passion and excitement.

o We seek out inspiration or allow ourselves to be inspired.

o We are truthful, gracious, courageous, compassionate, authentic.

o We realise something or have an insight.

o We gain a better understanding or increased clarity.

o We are able to quieten our thoughts and still our mind.

o We open to new experiences, new thoughts or new perspectives.

o We feel appreciation.

o We see the beauty and perfection around us.

o We reach out to and align with our Core Self.

We move away from our Core Self and flip into our Ego state, when we do the opposite of any of the above.

For the perspectives, desires and ways of operating of our Core Self to make sense to us, we have to listen with our heart. Our mind easily misunderstands and our intellect can only too readily pick holes into basically everything that has been said so far and I am going to say now. Everything can be twisted, turned on its head and misunderstood, particularly when it comes to characteristics of our Core Self. It requires a desire and earnest intention to arrive at a more intuitive and comprehensive understanding.

Therefore we need to read the list below residing in a centred space and listening with our heart in order for the distinctions to have meaning.

In order to function more closely in line with our Essence we need to be and do the following simultaneously:

We need to	And yet at the same time	We need to:
Pursue our work with great intent, determination, discipline and passion	and yet	Be relaxed, easy-going and detached from the outcome
Be forever changing	and yet	Be content and at peace with where we are at now
Be fully accepting of all our aspects and of all that we encounter	and yet	Strive to transform those aspects, which are not beneficial and change readily our unhelpful perspectives, attitudes and ways of being
Be patient with the process, with getting from here to there	and yet	Be insistent and persistent in pursuing the change
Be acutely aware of and sensitive to where the other person's reality is at and take that into consideration	and yet	Be loyal to and congruent with our own truth, understanding and to our own 'inner' calling
Require a great deal from ourselves	and yet	Be patient and compassionate with ourselves
Be totally accepting of our past choices	and yet	Leave our past behind and choose anew that which facilitates our goals and is in line with who we want to be
Be totally committed to our decisions and intentions	and yet	Easily change our mind in the face of new insights and understanding

In order to ensure that our choices, communications or actions are governed by our Authentic Self rather than by an Ego aspect we need to consider or examine before any decision our intentions and motivations. We need to ask ourselves:

Is this activity fear-motivated or love-motivated?

What is my intention here?

Does this comment, request, thought or action come from a place of goodwill, support, friendship or from a place of requirement, need, unresolved hurt, resentment, self-righteousness? If the action comes from the former place it will benefit us and the other(s). If the action comes from the latter place, it will cause further hurt, turmoil, limitation.

What am I trying to achieve here?

What are the consequences or effects of this action?

Is this in line with who I want to be?

Is this promoting my higher goals?

Is this enlarging or reducing, uplifting or depressing?

Is this benefiting or detrimental, helping or hindering, healing or hurting?

Our body sensations will greatly assist in discerning the most beneficial response, if we are not already sure. Feeling good, lively, elated, energised or experiencing a sense of rightness means, that the action or communication is Core Self-sponsored. Feeling dull, uncomfortable, drained, irritated or less than joyful means that our decision is governed by an Ego aspect.

We may also ask ourselves:

What is the most helpful, effective, sensitive, empathic way to respond or say this?

Which part of me is speaking now? The 'reactor', the 'victim', the 'creator', our 'empathic' aspect, the part which takes responsibility?

We need to get to a place, where we no longer act or speak on impulse, where we give some (at least a few seconds') thought before we interact or do something.

We also need to:

o Become alert, keen observers of all that we think, all that we say to ourselves, of our communications, our behaviour, our body language, of our attitude and our way of being.

o Become mindful of what we notice and pay attention to, the communications and the relationship dynamics which are displayed in front of us, the situations or incidents, which meet our approval or disapproval.

o Be conscious and aware of our desires and passion, the driving force behind our actions and communications.

o Do everything consciously, deliberately, purposefully rather than reacting by default to external stimuli.

o Create quiet, uninterrupted time to ponder our aspirations and goals, and how we would like to be. Then everything we say, think and do needs to fall in line with what we have decided.

o Organise our allocation of time and energy according to our priorities and put everything in place to follow through our decisions and intentions, to make them happen, to 'walk our talk'.

o Focus in others on the perfection of their Core Self rather than homing in, debating or judging the imperfections of their Ego or limited Self.

o Let go readily of all that no longer serves us and no longer represents who we want to be.

o Require ourselves to throw out all negative thoughts, to relinquish all self-pity, guilt, shame, regret, reproach, blame, to release all doubts, to transcend all fears, to transmute all pessimism.

o Embrace fully our role as creators and refrain from the disabling seduction of the victim role.

When we function in alignment with our Core Self:

We are contributing, supporting and benefiting others greatly. We are giving and receiving in balance. We become reliable, transparent and sincere. We are focused and deliberate in our actions and communications. Life has ceased to be a struggle; it has ceased to be full of hardship, emotional turmoil, suffering, difficulties, limitations, unpleasant experiences, disappointments or regrets. Life is infinitely fulfilling, exhilarating, worthwhile, blissful, peaceful and full of vitality. It has dignity, elegance and meaning. It is full of satisfaction, purpose and power and yet full of so much more, which is beyond words.

Appendix 1: Choice

Choice is a quintessential part of our human existence. To choose or not to choose is not an option. We cannot avoid choosing. Not choosing is as much of a choice as choosing proactively. Choosing without realising that we are choosing has the same consequences as an active, deliberate choice has.

Some of the critical questions are:

Which of our parts is doing the choosing or which part has the dominant vote?

Do we choose consciously and deliberately or unconsciously and haphazardly or by default?

Do we own our choices or do we deny that we made a choice?

Who is making the choice?

The question is basically, which of our aspects is in charge of a particular choice? Is the choice governed by our Core Self or one of our Ego entities? Is the choice love-sponsored or fear-sponsored? Is it motivated by our most rewarding goals and our highest good or by some past, unexamined conditioning or issue?

It is advisable not to make critical choices in the midst of a temporary difficulty or in the throng of intense emotions. Under those circumstances one of our Ego aspects is dominant and we are operating from a limited awareness or lower perspective. For a choice to be beneficial to ourselves and others it needs to be on course with our Essence. Therefore, it is useful to become clear about the source of our choice. A feelings of ease and elation will indicate whether a particular choice is compatible with our Core Self.

What we choose

We choose primarily our perspective, attitude or way of being, which in turn will elicit our thoughts (and the resultant feelings) and our actions. Additionally we decide who we want to be e.g. whether we want to be a person of integrity, patience, empathy or courage. Equally we determine our priorities, what is important to us and what is secondary. Furthermore, we decide our boundaries, what we are prepared to tolerate and what not.

How we choose

We may choose consciously or unconsciously, deliberately and purposefully or haphazardly and randomly, autonomously or influenced by others, in a Core Self manner or Ego directed.

When we choose unconsciously and haphazardly or without giving our choice some thought, we have no influence over the outcomes of our choice. The results of our unconscious choices may be, and often are, counterproductive to our goals or desires and may give rise to unwanted experiences.

Points of note with regard to our choices

o Each of our choices creates consequences and outcomes in terms of circumstances, events, conditions, feelings, experiences or responses from others. The results are immediate, intermediate or long term. We can always change immediately how we feel or how we are being through a change of mind, a choice to perceive and thus feel differently or a decision to be different e.g. to be content, to be happy, to be peaceful or to be in charge.

o Before choosing a particular action or communication we

need to be very clear and honest about what our decision involves and what the consequences are. Deluding ourselves about the probable outcomes or pretending that we don't know does not change the outcome. We need to embrace the known consequences, so that we can live with the consequences without anger, resentment, disappointment or sadness.

o It is not useful to classify choices as 'right' or 'wrong', 'good' or 'bad', because these terms are relative and only represent a judgement of the particular person using those labels. We are in no position to assess the potential overall benefit or detriment of a particular choice for the person doing the choosing. Each decision has its consequences and each consequence, however unpleasant and unwanted it may be, offers a whole range of new choices and brings with it the grand opportunity to move into greater freedom, power, peace and greater maturity. However, we may think of choices in terms of what serves us well and is on course with our intentions. Yet each choice has its merit, even the choice which appears to impede what we are trying to achieve, because each choice opens up a whole array of new choices with its multitude of possible benefits.

o It is worthwhile taking responsibility for our decisions. Pretending that we did not make a particular choice does not relinquish us from the responsibility for our decision nor does it exempt us from the consequences of our choice. We may deceive ourselves and others that we are the innocent victims of circumstances or others' thoughtless behaviour. It may appear that we gain, e.g. by way of sympathy, pity or exoneration, by blaming somebody or something for our unwanted experiences. However, by not acknowledging our part in what we experience, we lose heavily in terms of decreased freedom and power. We have to decide what is more worthwhile to us: pity or freedom.

o It is a popular belief that falling in line with the perception or action of a particular person, a group, a community or a whole population does not involve a choice on our part. The logic applied here appears to be that if somebody else of perceived authority or a large number of people carry out a particular activity or hold a particular judgement, any choice on our part is obviated and the action or opinion adopted by the others is seen as mandatory. However, just because we fall in line with a judgement which the whole world seems to hold, does not save us from the consequences of opting for that particular choice.

o It is more helpful to choose proactively what we want rather than making a choice to avoid what we don't want. In focusing on what we want we channel our energy towards that end. Conversely, when we focus on what we don't want, we inadvertently invest our time and energy on something which we want to evade.

Our birthright of free choice is a source of immense freedom and power and not to be squandered thoughtlessly. We cannot lose this birthright of free choice, but we can fail to use it consciously, knowingly, purposefully, beneficially, wisely. In making our choices we determine:

> Whether we create hell or heaven for ourselves;
> Whether we have chaos or peace in our life;
> Whether we are enslaved or free;
> Whether we are discontent and miserable or content and fulfilled;
> Whether we are prisoners of our fear or free agents of our love;
> Whether we are suffering or feeling joy;
> Whether we create pain or enjoy peace, freedom and exhilaration.

Appendix 2: Change

'Seek not to change the world. Seek to BE the change you wish to SEE in the world.' (Gandhi)

Change is an inevitable, given aspect of life. The only question is 'Which direction is change taking us?' Are the changes that are occurring in our life bringing us towards our goals, towards greater peace, fulfilment, freedom or not? Are they bringing us joy or pain, power or limitation, order or chaos, satisfaction or dissatisfaction?

It is worthwhile to determine and decide proactively, deliberately, with full awareness, which changes we opt for. If we do not approach changes consciously, they will occur according to our unconscious decisions and maybe in directions we may not like.

What we can and cannot change:

o We cannot change others. We can only change ourselves. We have morally and ethically no control over somebody else. So often we look to the other to change in order to bring about the change we wish to see. To this effect we may engage in manipulation and coercion. However coercion and manipulation violate the other's autonomy and right to choose and have negative repercussions such as resentment, resistance or reciprocal manipulation.

Instead we may use the tool of negotiation to accomplish a win-win solution. Alternatively we have the option to make the relevant changes within ourselves such as changing our perspective or our attitude, transforming a belief or acquiring a new skill. Usually to change a situation we have to make some changes within ourselves. At times, this is all that is possible.

o We can only deliberately change what we are aware of, acknowledge and own. We can only change what we make our own.

o We may change what does not work for us with something that does work. We may release what hurts and adopt that which elates. We may drop what is dysfunctional and promote that which moves us closer to the realisation of our aspirations.

Change being Ego- or Core-sponsored

Often change is approached with the impetus and force of anger behind it in order to overcome possible feelings of guilt, fear or doubt or to drown out any pain the change may incur. We have to find fault before we allow ourselves to alter a situation. We feel obliged to justify to the outside world, and maybe to ourselves, our wish to experience something differently. This method to bring about a change is Ego-sponsored.

However, should we decide that we are entitled to change our mind or should we acknowledge that, if a change is in our best interests, then it is also in the best interests of the other(s), then we give ourselves permission to make the desired changes and guilt is not an issue. Thus we may affect the change from our Centre or Core Self. Then we engage in clear, unambiguous communications and rational negotiations to elicit a win-win solution. We respond with empathy, without being manipulated by tantrums or upsets of others. We effect change with integrity, respect, compassion, from our centre of power and strength, rather than coming from weakness.

Change and what may be involved

Some changes occur spontaneously, without any input. Some changes require very little effort, just a mere decision. Other desired changes require a huge amount of perseverance in order to generate the required momentum to overturn something that has been practised and reinforced over a long period of time. Change may be perceived as quite inconvenient. It may evoke considerable fear, anxiety or doubt.

Thus change may require:
o willingness, conviction, considerable motivation and enthusiasm
o strong commitment, resolve and intent
o sustained input and effort and yet allowing the process to occur in its own time
o honesty and sincerity in order not to deceive ourselves
o that we are creative, inventive, inquisitive in order to find a method which works for us
o patience and constant repetition in order to overcome something which has been acquired over a long period of time.

We need to invite and embrace change. Change opens the doors to unimagined possibilities. It enables healing, growth, expansion. This in turn brings increased freedom, peace, ease, fulfilment, joy.

Appendix 3: Perception, meaning, experience

Perception, meaning and experience are interrelated and form a triangular relationship. Our experiences are created by how we perceive something and the meaning we give that particular occurrence.

Perception

What we see is shaped or modified in line with our 'reality'.

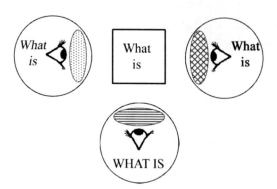

We often see or notice something through a filter. This 'perception' filter consists of our (often unconscious) beliefs, ideas, perspectives, fears or issues, which we have adopted in the past and which form now our 'reality'. Our perception filter screens out all that does not fit our beliefs or 'reality'.

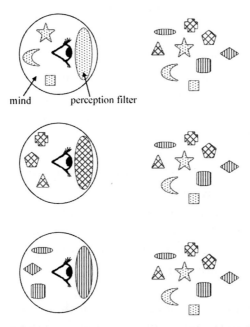

We notice and observe what we expect to see, especially when our filter contains a significant amount of unconscious data. What we do not expect to see, we overlook or ignore. Elements of our environment or occurrences do not significantly register in our awareness, unless we are at a stage where we are sufficiently conscious and our filter is significantly transparent.

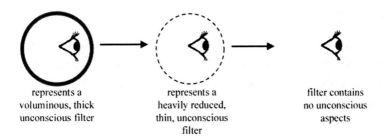

Yet we can reduce the unconscious aspect of our filter, until eventually all the unconscious parts have become conscious and we are aware of the whole content of our perception window; we are aware of what we are aware of. From here on we can increase our awareness without limits.

We may decrease the unconscious aspect of our filter:

o by applying the process and making use of our emotions or by what we observe in the 'mirror'.

o using the meditative, reflective approach, in which we either
seek out quiet time, reducing the chatter of our mind, which in turn allows new insights and understanding to filter through or
actively reach out and endeavour to get in touch with our Core Self (see Part 3). This again in turn modifies and diminishes the unconscious part of our filter through insights and accessing our innate knowing.

o by keen, reflective observation of our thoughts and all that captures our attention. This includes all spoken and written words, all interactions, behaviour, attitudes, relationships and occurrences.

o by embracing the concept, that nothing has any meaning except the meaning we give it. Thus we are no longer deluding ourselves that what we see or experience has nothing to do with us and we acknowledge the freedom and power to change our perception at any time. This attitude causes us to question our assumptions and judgements and to invest some reflection and thought into the meaning we give something. This results in greater awareness and less unconsciousness.

Meaning

Once we have noticed something or it has passed through our filter, we either reinforce a previously given meaning or we adopt a new one. The meaning we have opted for in turn modifies our filter. This generates a circular process:

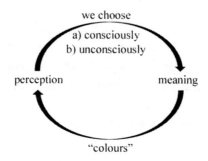

Each meaning we adopt reinforces or changes aspects of our filter. When we choose again and again a particular meaning, then the filter remains unchanged in content, but increases in quantity in this area. When we adopt a different meaning our filter becomes modified and the previously adopted meaning becomes less prominent.

The process of adopting a meaning may be done:

a) **unconsciously**, without being fully aware that we are making an interpretation. It may seem as if we are just observing what is so and we are not in any way contributing, *or*

b) **consciously**, in which case we are fully aware of what we are doing and we are clear that we are making a choice and nothing but a choice.

Meaning and choice

I have already mentioned several times that we choose the meaning we give a particular situation or event. A particular meaning is not a given or a foregone conclusion which is out of our hands.

Given that we choose all the meanings we adopt, we might as well choose, with purpose, meanings which benefit us and serve us well, which are on course with our wishes, aspirations and goals and in line with who we want to be.

It is also essential, in my opinion, that we ensure that we decide what something means independently, that we do not automatically, without examination and questioning, take on board the chosen meaning of others. The meaning others give is their business. The meaning we give is our business.

Meaning and responsibility

The significance of the above is that:

a) the meaning we give something is our responsibility and our responsibility alone *and*

b) the meaning others give is their responsibility.

However, it is our responsibility to clarify for others the meaning we attach to a particular word, comment, situation, action or relationship. We must ensure that the other person or persons are absolutely clear about what we mean and understand when we say such and such, how we interpret a particular incident, behaviour, response or comment.

Meaning and experience

Meanings and interpretations are creative. They create our experience. The meaning we give a comment or action determines how we are going to feel about it. The process is circular:

There is a dance between the two and the cycle continues, until we purposefully intervene with reflective awareness. Past meanings lead to present meanings and experiences, which in turn induce future meanings and experiences, unless we intercept with conscious awareness. That is, we become aware of the meaning we have given something, and then, if that meaning does not serve us well, we change our mind. Thus we intervene in the cycle of experience and meaning and ensure that we do not experience the same again and again.

Meaning and empowerment

Once we have embraced and integrated into our being the concept that we give everything its meaning, we have become independent of the communications, behaviour or actions of anybody else. It gives us total power over our experiences. We only depend on our own thoughts, beliefs, attitudes. How liberating is that? How freeing? It never fails to amaze me. I find it magnificent and exhilarating beyond description.

It may take a while to integrate this idea at a deeper level, so that it becomes more a matter-of-fact, authentic part of us. However, the rewards are enormous and make any effort worthwhile.

Appendix 4: Ego versus Core Self

Comparing and contrasting key words exemplifying the characteristics of the Ego and the Core Self:

Ego:	Core Self:
Being who we imagine we are	Being who we truly are at the Core
Being at the effect	Being at the cause
Creativity impaired, being influenced by others or by own impeding aspects	Creativity in full flow
Contracting, decreasing, closing down	Expanding, enlarging, opening up
Stagnant	Evolving
Apprehensive, tense, anxious, in turmoil	At ease, relaxed, at peace
Worried, heavy-hearted	Carefree, light-hearted
Easily takes offence; defensive	Does not take offence; no need to defend
Pedantic, small-minded	Generous, broadminded
Competitive	No need to compete
Suffering	Non-suffering
Hangs on	Lets go

Perceives lack; a sense of not enough; feels deprived	A sense of abundance; feels well provided for
Lack of appreciation due to lack of understanding	Appreciative, grateful
Dissatisfied, unfulfilled	Content, fulfilled
Thoughts, communications, actions are fear-sponsored; the domain of phobias, compulsions, addictions	Thoughts, communications, actions are love-sponsored
Perceives failure	Failure does not exist; anything can be gained from
Limitation, restriction, possessive of others	Freedom
Limited access to internal power; therefore resorts to external power	Full access to internal power; no need to exert external power
Loving conditionally	Loving unconditionally
Making conditions, withholding acceptance	Accepting all
Rigid, unresponse-able	Flexible, adaptable
Chooses and acts unconsciously and haphazardly	Chooses and acts consciously and deliberately
Often other-determined	Self-determined
Choice and action are usually not beneficial to self and others; usually a drain on others	Chooses and acts beneficially to self and others; contributing greatly
Unavailable to others	Available to others
Contains unconscious parts	Fully conscious and aware
Body of misconceptions, outdated conclusions, misinterpretations	Embodiment of innate knowing
Confused, uncertain, full of doubts	Completely clear

Incongruent; contradiction between thoughts, words and actions	Congruent; thoughts, words and actions are aligned and at one with each other
Deceitful, devious, hidden agendas	Honest, transparent, visible, high integrity
Seeks approval	Is independent of approval of others
In denial	Sees and confronts what is
Lacks confidence, because it is unaware of own intrinsic qualities	Confident, because it appreciates its own intrinsic qualities
Attached to outcomes	Not attached to outcomes
Unreliable	Reliable
Reactor	Creator
Feels superior or inferior	Neither feels superior nor inferior; sees itself as equal
Disconnected, separate, lonely	Connected, intimate, at one
Apprehensive and resistant to change	Embracing and living change
Closes down	Opens up
Has many needs	Has no needs
No real giving, no real receiving	Giving and receiving in balance
Giving with ulterior motive	Giving freely and to the greatest benefit of others without ulterior motive
Often not owning own choices, not taking responsibility for them	Fully owning own choices, taking full responsibility
Spends a large amount of time in thoughts of the past or the future	Focused mainly on the present, the here and now
Feelings of guilt, shame, regret	Free of feelings of guilt, shame, regret

Its existence has reduced purpose or meaning	Its existence is full of purpose and meaning
Holds back, impedes, contaminates	Supports, contributes, increases
Priorities are not well-defined and clear, time and energy are used haphazardly and often unconsciously; is easily distracted	Priorities are well-defined, clear, deliberate and pursued consciously and with full focus and zeal
Seeks answers and solutions outside of itself	Seeks answers and solutions within itself
Exclusive	Inclusive

Epilogue

Writing a book was the last thing I ever expected I would do. In my school days writing an essay was often a horrendous nightmare. Later writing letters or any other articles, especially official ones, were a laboured and much dreaded affair.

In order to write this book I had to overcome a powerful phobia of committing something of relevance in writing, amongst other obstacles. After holding my first workshops I realised that it would be useful to assemble the accumulated material in book form. Yet at the thought of writing a book I was struck by a great sense of trepidation. 'I can't possibly write a book' I told myself and yet I knew it was an important step in order to pursue on a larger scale what I so wanted to do and in order to respond to an intense inner yearning.

After the initial shock and resistance, I decided that I am not going to be held hostage by my old fears and issues. So I worked with that part that had such tremendous reservations. Doubts and fears surfaced many times during the writing; doubts that my book will not be worth reading or that it won't hold its place next to all the other brilliant books already out there. Again and again I had to work with my issues in this area and affirm and assert, in the face of those powerful doubts, my initial decision to create this book.

Another challenge in writing this book was that I had to present in a sequence of separate parts something that in essence is one whole, complete entity. I had to dissect what in substance is one. In order to fully grasp and appreciate one part, we have to already know and understand the other parts. However, to present a concept or notion word by word, sentence by sentence, we have to start somewhere and build up the whole picture step by step, analogous to the way a computer printer prints out a page line by line.

This generated a great deal of repetition. However, repetition powerfully promotes assimilation of the subject matter and is thus immensely useful. In this context it is important to point out that *Change Your Mind* needs to be read more than once in order to gain maximum appreciation and integration of all the finer points contained in the script. Therefore it is enormously worthwhile to read parts of the book or the whole book many times.

Both, my inner 'work' as described in the book, and the creation of this book have been an immensely fascinating and rewarding voyage of discovery and a path to enormously increased clarity for me. It seems to me now that I have written this book so that I grasp and assimilate the material at a profound level.

Although I still have an Ego landscape, I am nonetheless extremely happy with where I am at. I now experience such a profusion of joy, passion, fulfilment, gratitude and love that my heart sometimes almost bursts with it. I can see the perfection and sheer beauty in everything that has happened in my life. A lot of what I have encountered, I experienced as painful and unwelcome at the time. Yet it has brought me to where I am now, which is such a brilliant place to be. It has afforded phenomenal insights and learning and yielded deep knowing and wisdom. It has promoted a perspective which allows me to stay most of the time in a place of peace, whatever the circumstances and events, and to experience tremendous freedom and internal power, in total contrast to my earlier years. What I have gained is beyond description. Most of all I value immensely the profound, totally intimate, enormously inspiring and meaningful relationship with my Core Self. It is the singular most influential factor in the quality of my life.

My dearest wish is for everybody to enjoy this profusion of satisfaction, peace, happiness, and above all freedom and inner power. I salute you for embarking on this fascinating journey of discovery and awareness. I applaud all that you have brought and bring to light. I delight in your victory over limitations and I rejoice in your freedom. I encourage you to find the world inside of you and to discover the fullness of your beauty, worth, perfection, stillness, joy, power, fulfilment and absolute clarity.

If you are interested in further information on the subjects raised in this book or if you would like some assistance in any specific area or with some issues or challenges, I am offering private one-on-one and group consultations. Please enquire at the address below.

I am also holding workshops, which expand on the material discussed on these pages.

One set of workshops deals with the most effective and beneficial use of our emotions. The other set of workshops concentrates on the fine-tuning of the various methods (in particular the direct approach method) of profoundly connecting with our Core Self and residing more prominently in our Core state.

For further information regarding the workshops or for any questions or comments please write or email to the addresses below or visit the website:

E-mail : claritee@dsl.pipex.com
Website: www.clariteeonline.co.uk
Address: Johanna Claritee
P.O. Box 209
Cleckheaton
BD19 9BD
England

In Appreciation

First and foremost I want to acknowledge and thank my most supportive, accepting, loving, empowering friend, my Essence or Source. I value and enjoy beyond measure our relationship and the experience of your presence. The idea for this book came from you, as did all the inspiration and insights. I am grateful beyond words for the learning, understanding, epiphanies and elation the writing of the book has afforded me.

In addition I deeply thank my two daughters, Michaela and Gabriella, for their interest, support and sense of humour. I appreciate your understanding and assistance whilst writing this book and I am very proud of you. In particular a huge thank you to Michaela for producing for me so professionally and brilliantly all the diagrams and the title page.

A big thank you to Derek for your valuable, practical assistance and for being such a brilliant mirror for me. You provided me with endless food for thought.

I would also like to thank my extended family for all the learning you have provided and the love that you have extended to me. I especially thank you, Mutti and Vati, for your care and love; I hugely appreciate all that you have provided and facilitated. I also thank my brother for the generosity and kindness he has shown me over the years.

I thank Relate for the priceless awareness group sessions, which formed part of their training. I appreciated them immensely and they spurred on my search for greater awareness. I would like to see awareness sessions play a more prominent part.

Equally, I want to express my gratitude and appreciation to

Miles, Fiona and Rachel for their dedicated and professional efforts in transforming the rough manuscript into such a brilliant form.

I also want to acknowledge and express my immense gratitude towards the brilliant and inspiring teachers and wise beings whose examples promoted positive shifts and increased my understanding. Amongst them are Deepak Chopra, Gary Zukav, Neal Donald Walsh, Eckhart Tolle and Abraham. This is a short list of those who have particularly touched me.

Last but not least I want to acknowledge and thank all those who have helped me, knowingly or unknowingly, to get to know myself better, and all those who have inspired me with their examples, their attitude and their way of being. I am also deeply grateful to all those who allowed me to make a difference.

I am extremely grateful to you, the reader of this book, for all that you gain from this book. That is why I have written *Change Your Mind* and it fulfils one of my dearest wishes.